STOCK CAR RACING

JIMMIE JOHNSON

A DESERT RAT'S RACE TO NASCAR STARDOM

RON LEMASTERS, JR.
AND THE EDITORS OF
STOCK CAR RACING MAGAZINE

WITH PHOTOGRAPHY BY
NIGEL KINRADE

MOTORBOOKS
INTERNATIONAL

This edition first published in 2004 by Motorbooks International, an imprint of MBI Publishing Company, Galtier Plaza, Suite 200, 380 Jackson Street, St. Paul, MN 55101-3885 USA

The information in this book is true and complete to the best of our knowledge. All recommendations are made without any guarantee on the part of the author or Publisher, who also disclaim any liability incurred in connection with the use of this data or specific details.

We recognize that some words, model names and designations, for example, mentioned herein are the property of the trademark holder. We use them for identification purposes only. This is not an official publication.

Motorbooks International titles are also available at discounts in bulk quantity for industrial or sales-promotional use. For details write to Special Sales Manager at Motorbooks International Wholesalers & Distributors, Galtier Plaza, Suite 200, 380 Jackson Street, St. Paul, MN 55101-3885 USA.

ISBN 0-7603-2020-9

On the front cover: Jimmie Johnson got a once-in-a-lifetime chance in the brutal world of stock car racing when Jeff Gordon and Hendrick Motorsports decided that he was their racing future. *Nigel Kinrade*

On the frontispiece: Johnson's intense concentration helps him win on the ultra-competitive Cup circuit. *Nigel Kinrade*

On the title page: Lowe's finally saw its years of NASCAR car sponsorship pay off when the home improvement warehouse backed Jimmie Johnson. His driving often put them in victory lane. *Sam Sharpe*

On the table of contents: The No. 48 car in action. *Nigel Kinrade*

On the back cover: Johnson behind the wheel of his stock car and taking to the air in an off-road truck race. *Nigel Kinrade, Peter Biro*

About the author: Ron Lemasters Jr., an Indiana native, has been writing about NASCAR and other forms of motorsports since 1988, when he joined the staff of *National Speed Sport News*. Since then, the Ball State University graduate has been part of the NASCAR landscape as a writer, editor, and public relations specialist. His work has appeared in *Stock Car Racing* and *Circle Track* magazines, several International Speedway Corporation programs, and a variety of other motorsports publications. He and his wife, Chris, live in Concord, North Carolina, with their daughters Jordan and Devon.

Editor: Leah Noel
Contributing Editors: Larry Cothren, Glen Grissom
Layout by LeAnn Kuhlmann

Printed in China

CONTENTS

INTRODUCTION

A Two-Wheeled Start to Life on the Track

Jimmie Johnson, now 29, started his career at the age of four, racing motorcycles in the California desert. *Sam Sharpe*

Like many of today's top NASCAR stars, Jimmie Johnson began his motorsports career early—before he entered kindergarten. Starting when he was just four years old, he and his family pulled his vehicle to tracks all across California and the Southwest, unloaded, and went racing, just like thousands of youngsters do every year all over the country. Of course, being a native of El Cajon, California, there was a better than even chance Johnson was racing something other than quarter-midgets or go karts like most of his contemporaries. Being on the West Coast, where motorcycles are as popular as cars, he began his racing career on two wheels rather than on four.

His family, led by father Gary and mother Cathy, was one of those racing families that seem to dot America's motorsports world: They believed that racing is the main thing, not winning or getting the biggest trophy. Johnson looked up to his father, who was a mechanic on a desert buggy and his father's varied racing interests soon rubbed off on him.

When Johnson was 15, the Mickey Thompson Stadium Off-Road series began cranking up in a big way, so Gary Johnson arranged for his son to get a tryout with a five-buggy Superlite team. At the time, Gary was working for BFGoodrich as a truck driver on the West Coast and he asked BFG's Dan Newsome for some help in getting his son a shot.

That shot paid off as Jimmie Johnson became the youngest driver in Mickey Thompson Entertainment Group (MTEG) history that season. The following year, he got a ride in the second Chevrolet-backed Grand National Truck in the showcase division of the MTEG. A star was born.

As the young Johnson began to be more and more successful, his parents decided that he should focus on staying loose and having fun on the track. "If I ended up never getting here, they still would have been very proud of me and happy of what I tried to do," Johnson said of his family, which includes brothers Jesse, also a racer, and Jarit. "That's the thing with my parents . . . they just want to see you work hard and where you land is cool. It's all about working hard."

Hard work is the hallmark of Johnson's career. Back then, he was successful, yes, but he also had fun, something that many other racing parents seem to miss the importance of. "I'd watch these

Johnson was the youngest driver in the history of the Mickey Thompson Stadium Off-Road Series. Here he is in 1995 during driver introductions. *Centerline Photography*

Jimmie graduated to the Grand National Truck Series of the MTEG series in 1992. Here, he sails over the bumps on the floor of the Los Angeles County Coliseum. Note the severe camber of the front wheels on his Chevy Truck. *Pete Biro*

He quickly became a phenom in the Stadium Superlites class of the off-road series. *Pete Biro*

parents that would force their kids to win, force them to jump the big doubles, force them to do all this stuff, and my dad would be over there leaning up against a tree whistling at us as we went by.

"If we got off the bike and we'd tried as hard as we could, he was fine. It didn't matter where we finished. That's been something I've been extremely lucky about—that my parents took that approach with us."

Flush with the guiding principles supplied by his parents, Johnson entered the world of off-road racing as a teenager. Three straight stadium titles led to Johnson's desert racing for John Nelson and the Herzog family. That latter association, along with the careful consideration of Chevrolet's global racing boss Herb Fishel, carried Johnson all the way to Winston Cup. The Herzogs, led by father Bill and sons Stan and Randy, owned the vehicles Johnson drove from 1996 through 2001, when he quickly rose through the American Speed Association and Busch ranks and became a driver that everyone in NASCAR has their eyes on.

— Ron Lemasters Jr.

THE EARLY ROAD TO THE TOP

Off-Road Racing and the ASA are Short Pit Stops Along the Way

If there's an 800-pound gorilla in today's motorsports world, it's NASCAR. Every racing driver wants to be there, racing Nextel Cup on Sundays for the big bucks, the media exposure, and the chance to drive right into the record books as the best there ever was.

Jimmie Johnson was no different. As a youngster growing up in California, Johnson knew he wanted to be a Winston (now Nextel) Cup racer. The difference between the soft-spoken son of a racing father and the vast majority of racers who never do make it to racing's top level is the way in which he accomplished that goal.

Johnson's path to stardom started early—very early. He first tackled the rough-and-tumble motocross world at the age of four. Off-road racing—as much a staple of the southern California landscape as palm trees, surf boards, and smog—was his next stop on the path to becoming a stock car superstar. Finally, with the help of his off-road team owners, Stan and Randy Herzog and Herb Fishel of General Motors, Johnson entered stock car racing at a high level, in the short-track series of the American Speed Association (ASA). ASA was the crucible in which champions such as Alan Kulwicki, Darrell Waltrip, Rusty Wallace, and Mark Martin were forged.

Jimmie Johnson has always looked the part of a professional racing driver. He's posing beside his Chevrolet truck, which he used to win two straight Winter Series titles in CORR—a racing series that took up where the Mickey Thompson Series left off by offering off-road racing to the masses. *Centerline Photography*

From there, Johnson took the next step in his road to Nextel Cup stardom by tackling the NASCAR Busch Series (NBS). He finished seventh in his first NBS start, at the historic Milwaukee

Mile in Wisconsin, and he won the inaugural event at Chicagoland Speedway the following season.

His performance, both on and off the track, caught the eye of four-time Winston Cup champion Jeff Gordon. In the midst of his fourth championship season, Gordon, who had earlier signed a lifetime contract with Hendrick Motorsports, was on the lookout for a young driver he could field in a Hendrick car for a team he would own a piece of, and Johnson was that driver.

The interesting thing about Johnson's meteoric rise through the ranks to the zenith of American motorsports is that once he began racing on asphalt instead of dirt, sand, and gravel he spent little time at each rung on the ladder: two years in ASA, followed by two seasons in the Busch Series. Then he reached the promised land.

When he traded in his motorcycle for a 1,600-cc buggy in the Mickey Thompson Stadium Off-Road Series, he was only 15 years old. The following season, he graduated to the powerful Grand National Truck division, where the battles are bitter and hard fought. Enter Herb Fishel, whose eye for talent rivals any movie scout or corporate recruiter. He saw something in the clean-cut, clearly talented young Californian. As head of worldwide racing for Chevrolet, Fishel was constantly on the lookout for talented young drivers to install in various programs around the world, and Johnson fit the bill.

"A lot of people know Herb for keeping an eye out for young drivers," Johnson said back in 1999, as he was about to make the jump to the Busch Series. "He expressed interest in me when I was sixteen, and he's so deep in motorsports [that] he knows what's happening at all times and he has my best interests at heart. With my background and upbringing, there have been a few people that have made this possible, and Herb's one of them."

As a regular for the Chevrolet factory team, Johnson won three straight Mickey Thompson Stadium Off-Road titles. Here, he runs flat out around a corner. *Centerline Photography*

Even as a teenager, Johnson was no stranger to victory lane. Here, he's hoisting a Mickey Thompson Stadium Off-Road Series trophy for winning the Grand National Truck event. *Centerline Photography*

In addition to a slot in a factory-backed Chevrolet truck for the stadium series, Johnson was being groomed for bigger things. Public relations training, public speaking courses—it all came with the territory, and Johnson threw himself into them, applying the same tenet of hard work that had brought him there.

From here, it was up to Johnson where he wanted to go. First things first, however: Johnson had to prove himself in the stadium series before his other goals were broached.

A young Johnson pulls himself together in the cockpit of his Chevrolet truck. *Centerline Photography*

Out of the truck, Jimmie was a fresh-faced newcomer under the wing of GM's global racing boss Herb Fishel. *Pete Biro*

Off-road racing is meant to happen in the desert, like the sands in Arizona. Here, Johnson hustles a somewhat battered Chevrolet truck through the desert around Parker, Arizona. *Centerline Photography*

After making a splash in the stadium, Johnson went out to the desert with the SCORE racers. Here, he tops a rise, hard on the gas of his Chevy. *Pete Biro*

In the stadium series, Johnson won three straight Grand National Truck Series titles (1992–94), captured the Short-Course Off-Road Enthusiasts (SCORE) Desert championship in 1994, and raced in the SCORE Trophy Truck Series in 1995. He won the 1996 and 1997 Short-Course Off-Road Drivers' Association (SODA) Winter Series titles, and then it was time to leave the desert for the Midwest and ASA racing.

When he came to the ASA in 1998, Johnson was untested as a stock car driver. So far, his driving talents had been best showcased in the deserts of the Southwest, ripping through sand and rocks at better than 140 miles per hour in a howling, full-sized Chevrolet truck. Coupled with his experience on motocross bikes, the young man had learned a thing or two about car control from

Also after his stadium series stint, Jimmie raced in the Short-Course Off-Road Drivers Association outdoor series, which is based in the upper Midwest. Here, he flies over the hills of Wisconsin. *Pete Biro*

Johnson won the 1996 and 1997 SODA Winter Championship Series titles, and he celebrated many victories in front of the crowd. *Pete Biro*

Sitting on top of the world, Jimmie poses with his SODA championship-winning Chevy that he drove in 1997. *Pete Biro*

Jimmie noses his Chevy over the brow of a hill in a SODA race. To get an idea of the truck's suspension travel, note how the wheels are pushed up under the front fenders as the suspension prepares to launch the truck over the edge. *Pete Biro*

The SODA Series often had television coverage, for which Jimmie served as a guest analyst on many occasions. *Pete Biro*

those experiences. Still, controlling a big, heavy vehicle through wide-open spaces has little to do with close-quarters racing on asphalt. Contact among off-roaders usually has to do with hitting rocks or other desert detritus, not the quarter panels of your competitors.

Crashing has always been part of the oval-track racing scene, and given his relative inexperience, many racing observers figured that Johnson would crash a lot while learning the ropes. However, that did not happen because Johnson learned to take care of his equipment the hard way. He

The 19-year-old Johnson ready to race in Wisconsin in the Winter Series. *Centerline Photography*

Getting power to the ground is the name of the game, and Johnson is putting down some serious horses here at Crandon, Wisconsin, in 1997. *Centerline Photography*

Racing off-road is all about overcoming obstacles. Here, Johnson has all four wheels off the ground on his way to another victory.
Centerline Photography

Driving the Nelson & Nelson Chevy Trophy Truck, Jimmie rolls away from the starting gate for the annual Baja 1,000, perhaps the most famous off-road race since the demise of Le Carrera Panamerica, otherwise known as the Mexican Road Race. *Pete Biro*

Johnson, shown here hauling across the dry lake bed south of Mexicali, was involved in a whopper of a crash during the Baja one season, hitting a huge rock and flipping his truck into a wash. He spent the next two days there with around 100 race fans until his chase crew tracked him down. *Centerline Photography*

crashed during the annual Baja 1,000 in western Mexico while driving a Chevy Trophy Truck and spent two days with about 100 race fans at the bottom of a wash. "Ever since then, I've been really careful not to tear up my equipment," Johnson joked.

After a three-race get-acquainted campaign in ASA at the end of 1997, Johnson entered his rookie season in that series in 1998, driving the Herzogs' Pennzoil Chevrolet. His performance that year was solid: He finished fourth in the points and earned his fourth straight Rookie of the Year award (he had won them in the Stadium, SCORE, and SODA series as well).

While there are few absolutes in the world of motorsports, one tends to always be revered: If you can drive, you can drive, whether you're in a stock car on an oval track or banging around out in the desert with nothing but cacti and coyotes for company. It's all about that little part of your brain that tells your hands and feet how to react to save the other less capable parts of your body. One thing you learn about while driving around the desert at high speed is limits. Driving a stock car on fairly consistent surfaces is relatively easy when you're used to sand, dirt, and gravel. Driving on the limits is what it's about, and Johnson learned to be comfortable out on the ragged edge in a stock car.

Always a favorite of the media, Johnson plays to the crowd and the cameras at Memphis Motorsports Park following his first career ASA victory there in 1999. *ASA Archives*

In the following season, 1999, Johnson won his first two stock car events. He took the checkered flag at Memphis Motorsports Park and then won the season finale at North Carolina's Orange County Speedway—the last ASA race in history using the aluminum-block V-6 racing engines that the series had used since the early 1990s.

In 20 races that year, Johnson finished in the top five 11 times and in the top 10 a staggering 16 times, in addition to winning three poles.

He was now ready for prime time.

— Ron Lemasters Jr.

Signing autographs was something Johnson got used to at a very early age. Here he signs a 1997 hero card for a young fan. *Centerline Photography*

OFF ROAD AND ON TRACK

BY RON LEMASTERS JR.
Stock Car Racing, December 1999

Jimmie Johnson's Career Starts Going in Circles

Every driver has a victory dance. Johnson's first in a stock car came in 1999 at Memphis Motorsports Park.
ASA Archives

Jimmie Johnson came from the same background as Rick Mears, has the studied polish of Jeff Gordon and Tony Stewart, and has his sights set on a career as a stock car driver.

He's the latest sure thing to come from the fertile mind of Herb Fishel and the talent boffins at GM Motorsports, and he's spent the last year or two making Fishel look like the genius he is thought to be in racing circles.

Ask Johnson who he is, however, and you'll get a different reaction.

"I'm just a twenty-three-year-old kid from Oakland, California," he quipped.

While forgiving the young man for modesty, he's quite a bit more than that. He's the future—or at least a part of it—of NASCAR stock car racing.

Since he came to the American Speed Association's ACDelco Challenge Series in 1997 for a three-race stint, he's been one of those drivers everyone watches. Even while blowing off the sand and grit he accumulated after six years in the tough SCORE desert racing series and the now-defunct Mickey Thompson Stadium Off-Road Series, Johnson caught the eye of people who mattered.

One of them was Fishel, always on the lookout for fresh talent he can plug into one of the many General Motors racing programs. With the help of his father, Johnson was taken into the Chevrolet fold while still legally unable to hold a driver's license in some states.

"A lot of people know Herb for keeping an eye out for young drivers, and he's done it so much in the past," Johnson said of Fishel. "He's not someone I speak to every day, but I talk to him a lot. He seems like he's working every day to make sure I'm as strong as I can be, both inside and outside of the car. He's a really unique man. With my upbringing and background, there's been a few people who have made this possible, and Herb's one of them. If he hadn't, I'd still be sitting at El Cajon, doing what everybody else I graduated [from] high school with is doing."

Fishel found Johnson racing in the stadium off-road series and saw something in the youngster he liked.

"I started out in motocross, but I had one too many broken bones," Johnson said. "My dad, Gary, was into motorcycle racing growing up, so I got involved in that with him. At the same time, when I was getting older, he was a mechanic on a buggy that raced in the Mickey Thompson Stadium Off-Road circuit, and through his connections and his work, he got me into a class called Superlites. He got me in there to a test session for a team sponsored by BFGoodrich Tires. I got started at fifteen running the stadium series, and from there Chevrolet picked me up when I was sixteen, when they were starting to run a second truck in the stadium series."

Grand National Sport Trucks were the cream of the stadium series crop, and a 16-year-old kid driving one of them was certainly a novelty. "They started testing me for the ride, and I got it," Johnson said. "When I got involved with Chevrolet, they were interested in looking at and building a future, and I think Herb Fishel probably set that up the most. He's the one who presented me to Chevrolet. He really got the ball rolling at Chevrolet and had a lot of interest in me. I expressed to them where I wanted to go with my racing, and that was stock cars."

Johnson spends just another day at the office in his Chevy Truck. *Pete Biro*

The Herzog family—Randy, Stan, and Bill—know talent when they see it, as does General Motors' worldwide racing boss, Herb Fishel (center). Here, Jimmie (right) poses with Fishel and ASA teammate Rick Johnson (left). *ASA Archives*

Stock car racing is probably one of the tougher divisions in racing to break into these days, with NASCAR having its feeder systems designed to point the best and brightest to its premier divisions—the NASCAR Winston Cup, Busch Grand National, and Craftsman Truck Series.

Even so, ASA racing groomed a number of current Cup and BGN stars, including Mark Martin, Rusty Wallace, Kenny Wallace, Ted Musgrave, Dick Trickle, and the late Alan Kulwicki. It also had a hand in propelling drivers like Darrell Waltrip toward the limelight, even though it was a fledgling series some 30 years ago when Waltrip was on the rise. "That opportunity [to go stock car racing] happened for me in 1997 when I ran three ASA races with Bud Gebben's API team, which is who

Competition in ASA is routinely close, which makes it a good stepping-stone series for an off-road racer. Here, Johnson (No. 44) races with Midwestern veteran Russ Tuttle. *ASA Archives*

[1998 series champion] Gary St. Amant drives for," Johnson said. "They tested me and practiced me and took me to my first few races.

"At the same time, Herb Fishel and Chevrolet were discussing with the Herzogs about doing an ASA program and moving into asphalt racing. They've always been a real strong organization in off-road racing, and at that time I was driving their off-road truck. Herb saw them as the team for the future and me as a driver of the future and actually kind of guided us both to where we are now."

Where he is now is the top echelon of the extremely competitive ASA field, and he won his first race in series competition in June at Memphis Motorsports Park in Tennessee.

In five years, Johnson said he hopes to be among the elite in the NASCAR world, despite never having really considered that as an attainable goal growing up.

"I would hope to see myself in Winston Cup, being competitive. Dirt racing was everything to me as a kid growing up, and I'd see those NASCAR races on TV and I just didn't think it was possible for me to get there. Now it seems that it's become less of a dream and more of a reality. It's hard for me to figure out how it all happened to start with, but the racer in me—I want to move up.

"We're going to run the full Busch schedule next year, and I think we're going to be competitive there. I've always been able to win races wherever I've raced, and I want to win, not just go there

> *"Dirt racing was everything to me as a kid growing up, and I'd see those NASCAR races on TV and I just didn't think it was possible for me to get there. Now it seems that it's become less of a dream and more of a reality."*
>
> —Jimmie Johnson

Every driver loves to win the hardware, and Johnson's first piece in ASA was this trophy. *ASA Archives*

Victory lane celebrations can take on lives of their own. Here, Johnson's party is just cranking up at Memphis. *ASA Archives*

and fill the field. I want to go there and be competitive and run strong. We'll have some maturity with the team, and the Herzogs share some of the same goals I do as far as moving up and growing together. It's a long way to go and we'll see what happens. I just want to win races."

Winning races is what it's all about, and Johnson has adapted well to racing on tracks where the surface doesn't dry up and blow away like it does in the middle of the desert. His transition to the asphalt hasn't been without its worrisome aspects, however.

"Every track and track surface has its own rhythm, and asphalt is all about rhythm," Johnson said. "On the dirt, you've got things changing, as far as the cushion goes and the surface and all the rest. On asphalt, it takes awhile to find that and find it for each track."

The biggest challenge for Johnson was trying to maintain his concentration for three or four hours behind the wheel. "It's really a lot different inside the car, training your brain to be alert for two hundred and fifty laps. When I ran the desert series, you raced against the clock for twenty hours. The majority of the racing I've done, in the stadium series, has been fifteen-minute sprint races, and those were the long ones. So to go three hundred or four hundred laps at a whack was something I had to train myself to do.

"After a pit stop, even if it was the first one, I'd be thinking the race was almost over, even if we had three or four more [stops] to go. Being able to save the equipment, knowing that this might be the last time putting left-side

> *"I think with the testing that I've done in off-road tire testing, shock testing, and durability testing on the whole has made me very sensitive to the car."*
>
> —Jimmie Johnson

Two old motorcycle racers—many-time AMA Supercross title winner Rick Johnson (left) and Jimmie Johnson—compare notes on track conditions at Hickory (North Carolina) Motor Speedway. The two California drivers clicked as teammates because they had similar backgrounds and they communicated well. *ASA Archives*

tires on, maybe I'll have another set of rights, and when you spin the left rear tire you're also spinning the rights—just learning about all that. It's been a pretty steep learning curve."

Climbing mountains in stock car racing is much easier if you have someone like Howie Lettow in your pit box. The veteran chief mechanic is the unchallenged star maker in ASA racing, having groomed Musgrave, Bobby Dotter, and several other drivers for future stardom.

Johnson's experience in testing off-road setups and other forms of racing has helped bridge the gap as well.

"I think with the testing that I've done in off-road tire testing, shock testing, and durability testing on the whole has made me very sensitive to the car," Johnson said. "I'm able to relate things to the car and know exactly what the car needs. I don't know enough about the stock cars yet to know exactly what to do to fix it, but I'm learning that every weekend. I've been able to tell Howie what I'm feeling and we can work on it from there. While he's working on it, he's teaching me what I need to know to fix it."

One of the biggest influences on Jimmie's transition from off-road phenom to stock car prodigy was master crew chief Howie Lettow (right), who has made a career of molding younger drivers into champions. *ASA Archives*

There hasn't been much "fixing" involved in Johnson's ASA career, at least as far as wrecked race cars go. There's a reason for that, Johnson said, and it has to do with a very large rock, a failure in communications, and some Mexican off-road racing fans.

"It was at the Baja 1000, in 1995 or 1996, and I took down the eight-hundred-and-eighty-mile marker when I crashed," Johnson reflected with a rueful note in his voice. "I thought I could drive straight through. I was leading the race and I had a problem, threw the power steering belt and the oil pump belt off the truck. Then when we tried to start the truck, the starter motor was dead. We lost about an hour or so trying to get the truck back on the road. We got it back on the road, and at that point I figured I was out of the race, but I was still charging hard. Little did I know that the other two trucks that had passed me had broken down, which put me back in the lead.

"So I'm charging hard. I'd been driving for twenty hours then, hadn't slept yet. So I dozed off a little bit. I drove into a rainstorm that woke me up, and I was still on the track, but I was coming up on a turn. I was going way too fast for the turn. I tried to get it slowed down, but I knew I was going off the road, so I figured I better go off straight.

"When I plowed through everything, there was a rock the size of a Volkswagen Bug sitting there. I hit the rock and flipped and flipped. I'm down at the bottom of this little sand wash. You

Johnson pushes the Herzogs' Class 8 Truck hard through the desert in the early stages of the Baja 1,000. *Pete Biro*

Popping a wheelie in the Mexican desert, Johnson wrings the last bit of horsepower from his trusty desert pony.
Pete Biro

won't believe this, but there were about one hundred Mexicans at the bottom of this wash, with bonfires and their wives and everything, watching the race. A lot of times the people who watch the race like that go out and pull markers down and wait to see a crash.

"Well, they got to see their crash. I spent two days with those guys until the communication went to my crew guys. My chase truck had a problem and was broken down. By the time the chase truck for my teammate, Larry Raglund, got to me, it was almost two days later."

During that time Johnson did some serious ruminating on how the situation had come to pass.

"I had a lot of time to sit there and reflect," he said. "I drove for John Nelson, and John always wanted you to run hard.

"He really pushed me to charge hard in the stadium stuff. I was eighteen years old, wound up, ready to charge hard, and I got into a desert truck. You really have to have some experience to race those. You race the clock; it's an endurance race. After that crash, I really started reflecting on my style. Since that crash—and I raced two more years of off-road—I never had that truck upside down, and I've never torn anything up in stock cars."

Despite that, Johnson still considers himself an aggressive driver. "Ever since then, I've been on the right side of the aggressive line, where before I crossed it quite frequently and had been lucky enough to save it. But I think I've gotten a little older and a little more mature. I still feel I'm pretty aggressive."

Jimmie Johnson, ready to roll. Here, he prepares to roll off the grid prior to the start of his last ASA race—1999's season finale at North Carolina's Orange County Speedway. *ASA Archives*

Training for the oval tracks in the desert has helped drivers like Indianapolis 500 winners Rick Mears and Parnelli Jones, and it also has helped Johnson in certain ways.

"I think it's easier for a dirt racer to go race on asphalt than it is the other way around," he said. "In dirt racing, you learn to drive a car comfortably on the edge all the time. When you get in an asphalt car—if you adjust your style enough and drive that car properly—and when you get in situations, it doesn't bother you that much, and you can drive that way every lap. I can see why the dirt helps you."

What he couldn't prepare for, despite the fact he was racing in the middle of the desert, was the heat inside a stock car.

"In desert racing you never had a windshield, so you always had fresh air blowing across you," Johnson said. "Even out in the desert in the summer, like in Barstow, California, when it's one hundred and fifteen degrees out, when you're in the truck and the truck's moving, you're relatively cool. I'm hotter in the ASA car on a fifty-degree night than I ever was in the one hundred-and-fifteen-degree weather in the middle of the desert, so I've had to adjust to the heat. As hot as temperatures are in the Midwest with the humidity, I try to run in the middle of the day, throw on a sweatshirt and sweatpants, and get used to it that way."

The second of Johnson's two career ASA victories came in the 1999 season finale. *ASA Archives*

On his way to victory, Johnson leads Jack Landis (87) and ASA star Mike Miller (18) during the middle stages of the race. Miller raced for the season title with Tim Sauter, but lost the championship by a single point. *ASA Archives*

One thing Johnson, like any other stadium racer, doesn't have to adapt to as much as pure desert racers is traffic. It does take a little getting used to, but Johnson has a fix on it.

"The stadium racing I did is sort of like road course racing where you could set somebody up and you'd have a strong section of the track to pass them," he said. "In stock cars, you're always turning left, and it's really the same at either end. Learning how to pass in a stock car was difficult, but as far as running in traffic, I was used to that from my stadium experience. That's one thing I didn't quite care much for, racing in the desert. You'd chase somebody's dust cloud, bust through it, tap him once or twice, he'd move over, and you'd go on. You never really raced anybody for anything. That's part of what my problem was in the desert, too. I'd chase all the dust clouds and wouldn't drive my own race."

Driving his own race will come second soon to driving his career. He will have crew chief Tony Liberati in his corner next season. He'll also have a familiar face driving the transporter.

"My parents [father, Gary, and mother, Cathy] are moving to Charlotte soon," Johnson said. "My dad's going to drive the Busch hauler for us next year."

The elder Johnson has had a profound effect on his son's career, pushing hard to get him a ride with Jeff Bennett's Superlites team. "My dad drives the West Coast trailer for BFGoodrich, and Dan Newsome from BFGoodrich first gave me a chance to drive in Superlites with a five-car team sponsored by Nature's Recipe Pet Food," Johnson said. "Jeff Bennett owned the team, and Dan Newsome really leaned on Jeff to get me the ride. Well, my dad really pressured Dan to pressure Jeff Bennett."

It's a long way from the old stadium course at the L.A. Coliseum to the shining lights of Daytona, Charlotte, and Texas, but it won't be too long a run for the 23-year-old from Oakland, California.

He's been racing against the clock all his life, and it stands to reason he'll beat the clock to his ultimate goal of NASCAR Winston Cup racing.

FROM BUSCH TO THE CUP IN TWO YEARS

Finding Success Thanks in Part to a Four-Time Winston Champ

It was on July 4, 1999—the all-American holiday—that Jimmie Johnson made his debut in the NASCAR Busch Series. He finished seventh at the Milwaukee Mile in a Herzog Chevy, a considerable feat. He had raced at Milwaukee twice before in the ASA and had done well both times, but unlike most of his other competitors in that Busch race Johnson was still just a neophyte when it came to racing on asphalt.

By the time he left ASA to race full time in the Busch Series in 2000, Johnson had a total of 43 races under his belt—seven more than a full Nextel Cup season—and a little more than two seasons under his belt. The drivers who took the traditional road to the big time—street stocks, late models, a touring series or two—sometimes raced 43 times a season for several years before making the grade.

Still, with the Herzogs and carrying a sponsorship from Alltel, Johnson began his career as a

The Busch Series gives little time for contemplation. Here, Jimmie takes a moment during a hectic qualifying session.
Nigel Kinrade

Busch Series regular by missing the field for the season-opening race at Daytona. It was his first exposure to restrictor-plate racing on a 2.5-mile track, and the fledgling Herzog Motorsports team,

Running hard on the bottom at Rockingham, Johnson finishes 22nd in his first race as a Busch Series regular.
Nigel Kinrade

One of the challenges of Johnson's ascension to the NASCAR Busch Series was learning new tracks nearly every weekend. Here, Jimmie Johnson (92) battles with Busch Series regulars during his first race of the 2000 season. He missed the show at Daytona.
Nigel Kinrade

As Johnson moved up the ranks, the competition got a little tougher at each level. Here he races with Chad Little (97) at Darlington. *Nigel Kinrade*

led by crew chief Tony Liberati, had its work cut out for it when Speedweeks rolled around. Shaking off that somewhat disconcerting welcome to NASCAR, the team rebounded the following week at Rockingham by making the race and finishing a respectable 22nd. Johnson went on to finish 10th in the final points that season, earning six top 10s.

Most of the tracks he raced on that year were ones he had never seen, let alone driven. Because of Johnson's inexperience, he and Liberati worked out a program to get Johnson used to the tracks in the shortest amount of time possible. They unloaded the car on Friday morning and spent the first practice session getting Johnson acclimated. Liberati would put a setup on the car that was neutral, and Johnson simply drove to get comfortable, often following other drivers to learn the line. Then the fine-tuning began. It seemed to work, in part because of Johnson's ability and also because he and Liberati communicated so well.

The following season, Johnson and the Herzogs wore Excedrin colors on their Chevrolets and the team was a solid championship contender from the first week of the season. With one season under his belt, Johnson was able to start each weekend much farther ahead than he had in the past, and the results showed it. He ended up eighth in the final points, winning the inaugural race at Chicagoland. It was the only Busch Series race Johnson would win on his road to Winston Cup, but his solid performance, week in and week out, made the right people sit up and take notice.

One of those was Jeff Gordon, who came to see Johnson about halfway through the season. After a brief conversation with the soon-to-be four-time Winston Cup title winner, Johnson was on the way to join him as a teammate.

The rest, as they say, is history. But first, there was some unfinished business for Johnson in the Busch Series. Capitalizing on a rookie season that was as frustrating as it was successful, Johnson became determined to make a big step up his second year. During the off-season, he applied the lessons learned in the previous season and came up with the answers he needed to make that big step.

— Ron Lemasters Jr.

The thinking man's driver, Johnson always concentrates on the job that lies ahead. *Nigel Kinrade*

DRIVER'S SEAT

No More Headaches

BY JIMMIE JOHNSON
Stock Car Racing, March 2001

Editor's note: It's one thing to be good and get noticed by important people. It's another to have the next two years mapped out for you with the likes of Jeff Gordon and Hendrick Motorsports. Toward the end of the 2000 season, not only did Jimmie Johnson add to an already great Busch Grand National deal with Herzog/Excedrin Racing for this year, but he was personally chosen by Jeff Gordon to drive a Hendrick Winston Cup car in 2002. Now, life in NASCAR for the likeable Johnson is without the usual headaches.

There's definitely a lot going on. I was just thinking back where I was a year ago at this time. We had just run five Busch races and were looking forward to the 2000 season but didn't know what to expect. It seems like an eternity has gone by, but it's really only been about 12 months. I feel real lucky. I've kind of been saying to people that I've got the yellow brick road laid out in front of me, and I've just got to stroll on down it.

Jeff Gordon's been somebody I've always been able to just go up and talk to and [has] been really approachable. At Michigan, I went to him for advice on some opportunities that were being presented to me. And through that conversation with him, he had mentioned that there might be some changes coming at Hendrick Motorsports. There might be something where I would fit in the program. That led to some discussions with Rick Hendrick and with Jeff. Shortly thereafter, they had an offer for me on the table that was a dream come true—really.

They're building a new, 85,000-square-foot facility at the current complex.

One of the attributes that attracted corporate sponsors to Jimmie Johnson is his image. This is the picture of a successful, marketable racing driver.
Nigel Kinrade

Bristol (Tennessee) Motor Speedway is one of the toughest tracks in the world, yet Johnson showed quite an aptitude for it. Here he leads a series of Busch regulars during the spring race.
Nigel Kinrade

Jeff's going to be part owner in the program, and he's in the No. 24. So they're going to put both teams in-house in the same building, and Jeff's going to move his licensing company in-house and have everything there at Hendrick Motorsports.

They're going to utilize me in a lot of the tests. Simple functions tests—motor testing, brake testing, all that kind of stuff that they don't want to trouble their drivers with. You know, stuff that drives them crazy but stuff I'm really excited to do. I just need to get experience in a Cup car and on these tracks, and I've got an awesome Busch program to give me more experience as well.

Hendrick is working real hard to help our Busch program with some added help from the Herzogs. We just came off our rookie year finishing 10th—an exceptional year. We've got a commitment from Excedrin to run the Busch Series for this year. So we kind of all feel we're at the same level, looking forward to the same things. There were some hard times here, getting going with this decision, but everybody knew that this was something I couldn't turn down.

The Busch Series has its share of Nextel Cup drivers who run regular schedules. Here, Johnson leads Jeff Burton's Ford during a race at Michigan. *Nigel Kinrade*

And my owners, Stan, Randy, and Bill Herzog, as sad as they were because they wanted to move onto Cup together, they knew this was an opportunity of a lifetime. They've been like family to me for the last five years, taking me through racing around tires in the dirt to making my dreams come true in stock car racing.

There have been a lot of times where I thought I was crazy, sacrificing even from back in high school. But for some reason in the back of my head, I just was confident that things would work out. And they have. I've been able to chase my dreams and make all those sacrifices pay off. I was worried at the time: Boy, if racing doesn't work out, what am I going to have? If you just work hard enough at it, and you're a good person, well, good things happen to good people. That's what I pride myself on, and it's all turned out. So, I'm really looking forward to this year and not having to worry about anything. I'm just going to drive race cars.

Getting up to speed has never been Jimmie Johnson's problem. *Nigel Kinrade*

A ROOKIE NO MORE

BY RON LEMASTERS JR.
Cirle Track, June 2001

Jimmie Johnson Plans to Make the Most of His Sophomore Season in NASCAR's Busch Series

Jimmie Johnson is something of a prodigy. At the ripe old age of 25, he has been a motorcycle racing wunderkind, an off-road racing champion, rookie of the year in the American Speed Association, and one of the brightest youngsters to come around since Jeff Gordon first traded top wings for fenders.

As a matter of fact, Johnson's precociousness attracted the attention of the three-time Winston Cup champion last year—enough so that Johnson's maiden venture into the major-league series in 2002 will be run out of Gordon's shops at the massive Hendrick Motorsports complex near Lowe's Motor Speedway.

Last year, however, Johnson was the greenest of rookies on the NASCAR Busch Grand National Series. Going into the season, he hadn't even seen, let alone raced on, some of the tracks on the BGN schedule. Las Vegas Motor Speedway was one of those he'd never seen, but he did recognize the area.

"I raced all around the desert outside of there," he cracked one day last year. "So, I guess you could say I have raced in Las Vegas."

Despite being a very young stock car driver on a team making the jump from ASA to the Busch Series, Johnson and crew chief Tony Liberati fashioned a second-half run that saw them place 10th in the final standings. It is this string of solid performances that leaves Johnson with the idea that he and his Excedrin-sponsored Herzog Motor Sports team can be contenders from the get-go this season.

Johnson's second Busch Series season with the Herzogs saw a new sponsor in Excedrin.
Nigel Kinrade

"In one respect, we didn't want to stop racing last year because we were really starting to hit our stride," Johnson said. "But at the same time, now we all get to start over on a clean sheet of paper and go after the point situation again with that rhythm we had and the confidence and the feeling that we are able to be a contender week in and week out.

"I'm just looking to get started where we left off, and hopefully we can start running in the top ten consistently like we did at the end of last year," he continued. "Then we need to start knocking down those top fives, and once that comes, we'll be ready to win some races."

The 2000 season didn't start off exactly as Johnson, Liberati, and the Herzogs wanted; they missed the season opener at Daytona. That, Johnson explains, was as much a matter of expectations set too high as anything else. This season, if anything, the expectations are just as grand. The difference comes from having a season under his belt.

> *"I've been known during the off-season to do this transformation, where everything finally has a chance to soak in. I think about racing so much, there really hasn't been an off-season yet."*
>
> —Jimmie Johnson

Communication is the hallmark of every good racing team. Jimmie Johnson knows that and often confers with crew chief Tony Liberati (left) on changes for the race ahead. *Nigel Kinrade*

While weekends are jam-packed with on-track activity, there are times when there's nothing to do but sit around and wait. *Nigel Kinrade*

"I hope I'm not thinking too high again," he said with a laugh. "We got off to kind of a slow start by missing Daytona last year and picked up our momentum really about the midpoint of the year. We were able to come back to tenth in the points. Realistically, I think if we start where we left off last year, we would be a top-five team in the points and maybe a long shot for the championship."

That's a pretty bold prediction for a second-year team with a new sponsor, but Johnson has a precedent.

"I've been known during the off-season to do this transformation, where everything finally has a chance to soak in," he said. "I think about racing so much, there really hasn't been an off-season yet.

A year's worth of experience made all the difference for Johnson, as he was in contention all day long at Rockingham. *Nigel Kinrade*

When he first came to Lowe's Motor Speedway as a Busch Series rookie, Johnson was not a big fan of the 1.5-mile track he's racing on here. That would change in a couple of seasons. *Nigel Kinrade*

Flashing through the dogleg at Atlanta Motor Speedway, Johnson is hard on the gas. *Nigel Kinrade*

Playing the waiting game, Jimmie watches other cars during qualifying. *Nigel Kinrade*

Rush hour at Atlanta. *Nigel Kinrade*

> *"There isn't anything that gets a driver ready for Busch Grand National racing besides Busch Grand National racing. ARCA, ASA, trucks, any of that stuff is just a totally different animal."*
>
> —Jimmie Johnson

I'm thinking of tracks and what we did and going through my notes and setups. In ASA it worked this way. We came out of the box the next season and sat on the front row, and we were competitive immediately. I'm hoping that takes place again, and we have a shot at the championship."

The guesswork, as far as never having seen some of the places he'll race this year, has been removed.

Johnson and Liberati found a way to combat the driver's relative lack of experience, and it worked well during their second-half surge.

"At first, Tony was used to being with an experienced driver who could unload, come off the truck, and cut a qualifying lap," Johnson noted. "We tried that at the beginning, but I wasn't at that point to be able to cut a lap first time out because I'd never been there. What we started to learn to do, and fell into a really good rhythm with, was to kind of sacrifice that first set of tires. We're only given two sets of tires for practice, and that first set, we decided, was to let me go out and run five laps at a time to try and find my way around the track and make sure I was in the right spot. Then we'd spend the majority of practice getting me seat time and making small adjustments to the car. Then toward the end of practice, we'd stick the second set of tires on the car, make a qualifying run, and find out where we were. We found a lot more success in doing that instead of trying to unload and go fast at the beginning. It made me drive the track wrong and put too much pressure on us right off the bat. Going into this year, I've at least been to these places once and I'm hoping to speed that process up."

Already strapped into his seat, Johnson pulls on his helmet for another round of battle.
Nigel Kinrade

A fan favorite since he was a rookie, Johnson always receives a warm welcome from fans during driver introductions.
Nigel Kinrade

Although it is not as prevalent in the Busch Series, certain sponsors run a variety of special paint schemes during the season. The regular red-on-white paint scheme split time with the blue Excedrin PM colors (below).
Nigel Kinrade

Asked what his first piece of advice to a first-year participant in the Busch Series would be, Johnson went the basic route.

"The advice I would give to a young driver is to just be patient," he said. "There isn't anything that gets a driver ready for Busch Grand National racing besides Busch Grand National racing. ARCA, ASA, trucks, any of that stuff is just a totally different animal. It's not hard to get within a half-second, but to get those last few tenths . . . it just takes time. It takes time for you as a driver to learn those little feelings. The only way you work through all those feelings and know what makes the car faster and what makes it out of control is just with seat time. That's the biggest thing I had to go through.

"My desire and ambition, and those of my crew chief and the Herzogs, was so high. We thought we were going to be able to overcome not having a lot of experience. We did a lot in a short period of time, but man that was a hard first half of the year. We were beating our heads against the wall, wondering, 'Why are we not up front? We know that's where we need to be.' It just took some time."

Johnson was up on the wheel all season in 2001, finishing sixth in series points. Here, he races with Mike McLaughlin (48) and Tim Sauter (61) at Daytona in his first start on the big 2.5-mile oval. *Nigel Kinrade*

FROM THE DESERT TO DAYTONA

BY BOB MYERS
Circle Track, May 2002

Jimmie Johnson Is the Latest Young Talent to Climb the Mountain to NASCAR's Top Division

Jimmie Johnson has to pinch himself to make sure he's in the real world. Johnson, a blue-chip rookie, began his first full NASCAR Winston Cup season in February driving the No. 48 Chevrolet for a new Hendrick Motorsports team co-owned by Jeff Gordon and Rick Hendrick and sponsored by Lowe's Home Improvement Warehouse.

Most rookies could only fantasize about having four-time and reigning Winston Cup champion Gordon as a teammate and Hendrick as an owner, plus the vast resources of Hendrick Motorsports at their disposal. Hendrick's multiple teams have won five Winston Cup and three Craftsman Truck Series titles in the past eight years.

That Johnson signed his Winston Cup pact in September 2000 is all that really matters now, but how the deal came about is one for Ripley's.

For the past two seasons, Johnson drove Chevrolets for Herzog Motorsports in the NASCAR Busch Grand National Series. In July 2000, Alltel, the team's sponsor, announced it would not return in 2001. As a result, word traveled fast that Johnson might be available at the end of the season if no sponsor was signed. He began to receive a surprising number of overtures from Winston Cup, Busch, and truck series owners.

Though Herzog eventually signed Excedrin as sponsor for 2001, the uncertainty during the interim weighed heavily on Johnson. What should he do, and how should he handle his situation? All he knew for sure is that if forced to make a change, he would stick with Chevrolet. He first hooked up with Chevrolet when he was 16. Herb Fishel, General Motors' global racing chief, helped steer his career.

One of the biggest news stories of 2001 was the announcement that Johnson would drive a car owned by Rick Hendrick and Jeff Gordon in the Winston Cup Series in 2002.

Nigel Kinrade

The Lowe's team pushes Jimmie's car out onto the pit lane during the Brickyard 400 at the legendary Indianapolis Motor Speedway. *Nigel Kinrade*

A Crazy Idea

Johnson had what he calls a "crazy idea." Why not seek advice? How about Jeff Gordon, who had skyrocketed to fame and fortune and seemed to have done everything right, on and off the track?

Johnson didn't know Gordon beyond a hello. That was enough. At the drivers' meeting before the Busch race at Michigan Speedway in August 2000, someone sitting behind Johnson grabbed him by the shoulders and said "hello." It was Gordon, who competed in select Busch races at the time. Johnson had been trying unsuccessfully to work up enough nerve to ask Gordon for a few minutes of his time. This was his break.

After he qualifies, Johnson goes to his teammates to tell them what works and what doesn't. Here, he tells Jeff Gordon the fast way around Rockingham. *Sam Sharpe*

When Johnson and team owner Jeff Gordon are on the racetrack, it's every man for himself. Here, Johnson leads his boss (24) while Ward Burton (22), Tony Raines (74), and Jamie McMurray (42) race around them. *Nigel Kinrade*

Johnson asked Gordon to see him, and Gordon invited him to his hauler after the meeting. Johnson told Gordon he was seeking advice, but Gordon did most of the talking. To Johnson's utter surprise, Gordon told him that he and Hendrick were interested in him possibly driving for them down the road, and that Hendrick Motorsports planned to add a fourth Winston Cup team to be housed in a new facility with Gordon's four-time champion team: two cars, one team. Gordon went on and on, Johnson says, adding that he didn't want to build Johnson's hopes too high, but advised him to "hang tight."

Johnson was incredulous. "I can't describe my feelings when I walked out of that hauler," he said later. "I had gone in there confused, wondering, and searching for advice and had come out with the possibility of a ride with Jeff Gordon and Rick Hendrick. I was simply trying to look ahead, be smart at a young age, and make sure I was going to have a ride in 2001. I wanted to stay with the Herzogs, but if anything happened to the team, I had to be prepared."

Not incidentally, Johnson beat his future boss in the race, finishing sixth; Gordon finished seventh.

Johnson had met Rick Hendrick at a Chevrolet function some six years earlier. Johnson and Hendrick's son, Ricky, a promising young driver who advanced from Craftsman trucks to Busch this year, were friends who had met through racing. Johnson knew that Fishel had spoken highly of him in the past to Rick Hendrick, but Hendrick had said nothing to Johnson about a possible ride.

Gordon promptly informed Hendrick of his conversation with Johnson, and they decided to go after him immediately. In about a month, Johnson autographed the contract. In fact, his signing actually accelerated plans to get the new team on track for the full 2002 schedule.

Living in the Moment

"The timing wasn't exactly right for us, but we were so impressed with Jimmie we needed to get him before somebody else did," Hendrick said. "If you wait around when you see a guy who seems to have it all, the whole package, it's too late.

"It was much the same with signing Jeff [in 1992]. We saw the talent first and then built around him. Jimmie is the reason we sped up this deal. . . . He's very talented and sharp, his communication skills and feedback are incredible, and he's just a great individual. Chemistry has developed between him and Jeff over the past year, and I think what Jeff can offer as his teammate is a huge asset. Their driving styles are about the same. We're very fortunate to have Jimmie in the Hendrick stable. He's an excellent fit. I think he is one of the best, if not the best, to come along in a long time."

Gordon said Johnson wasn't hired because there was no one else available; he was the right man for the job. "I raced with Jimmie some in the Busch series, and I've gotten to know him personally," noted Gordon, listed as the team's official owner. "Not only am I very impressed with his talent, but the way he handles himself with sponsors, media, and fans. Today's Winston Cup driver has to have the whole package, and that's hard to find. I am very excited about what we have found in Jimmie. He is a young and aggressive driver and gets the most out of his car."

"The timing wasn't exactly right for us, but we were so impressed with Jimmie we needed to get him before somebody else did. If you wait around when you see a guy who seems to have it all, the whole package, it's too late."

—Rick Hendrick

The transporter is a driver's home away from home at the racetrack, and Jimmie spends some time on the back porch during the Homestead weekend. *Nigel Kinrade*

Drivers often engage in the time-honored practice of "bench racing." At right, Johnson chats with Busch Series rookie Greg Biffle during a lull in the action at Michigan Speedway, and below with Jeff Green at Homestead.
Nigel Kinrade

At 5 feet, 11 inches and 175 pounds, Johnson is physically larger than Gordon, but their clean-cut appearance, some of their features, and their engaging personalities are similar. They're both California natives, Johnson hailing from El Cajon and Gordon from Vallejo. Johnson is 26 years old; Gordon is 30. Of course, Gordon has won 58 Winston Cup races, while Johnson has won none.

A Head Start

With the addition of bright, young crew chief Chad Knaus, Johnson believes he and his team have a head start on the new season. He made his Winston Cup debut bittersweet because he ran

Jeff Gordon and Jimmie Johnson make a great winning team. They also relate to each other well because they have so much in common. *Nigel Kinrade*

impressively in the top four before making a rookie mistake and crashing out at Charlotte in October and also raced at Homestead-Miami and Atlanta.

"We've had more than a year to build equipment and shop relationships with all the people involved," Johnson said. Even though his debut in the UAW-GM 500 ended prematurely with disappointment, Johnson feels, based on overall performance, ". . . that I made the transition to Winston Cup and that I am ready."

Johnson's initial objective this year was to make the field for the first four races because going in there are no owner's points toward provisional starts. "From there, I just want to earn the respect of these guys," he said. "I want to show them that they can race side-by-side with me and have confidence in my ability. Looking at what past rookies have done—Earnhardt Jr., Matt Kenseth,

Getting a bird's-eye view of the competition, Johnson and Chad Knaus ponder strategy from atop the war wagon. *Sam Sharpe*

> *"I am very excited about what we have found in Jimmie. He is a young and aggressive driver and gets the most out of his car."*
>
> — Jeff Gordon

Johnson waiting for his turn to qualify at Michigan. *Nigel Kinrade*

Tony Stewart, and Kevin Harvick — I think I will have every opportunity to be as successful. I'd certainly like to top Harvick's two wins [in 2001]."

"If Jimmie is competitive, qualifies in the top twenty, and shows he has the potential to win, that's as much as I'd expect the first year," Hendrick added.

Rapid Progress

Johnson has earned a crack at stock car racing's premier series. He raced through the minor leagues on motorcycles and in off-road buggies and trucks and American Speed Association (ASA) and NASCAR Busch Series stockers to get here.

Given that he has raced stock cars for only four years, his progress has been rapid. Johnson joined Herzog Motor Sports, led by Bill Herzog and his sons, Stan and Randy, in 1996 and drove their off-road trucks for two seasons. Johnson, with the blessings of Fishel and Chevrolet, moved with the Herzogs to ASA stockers in 1998, purchasing a Milwaukee-based team.

Led by Tony Liberati, the Herzog Motorsports crew gives quick service during the annual fall race at Phoenix International Raceway. *Nigel Kinrade*

Johnson knew nothing about stock cars. He moved his residence to Milwaukee to spend more time with crew chief Howie Lettow, a top ASA wrench whose students included Mark Martin, Ted Musgrave, and the late Winston Cup champion Alan Kulwicki. "The transition was huge for me," Johnson said. "I give Lettow all the credit for bridging the gap and teaching me the basics. He could explain complicated things so simply. From there, I was able to grow."

In the ASA, Johnson won two races and finished fourth and a close second in the championship standings. While maintaining a full ASA schedule, Johnson broke into NASCAR in 1998 with three Busch series starts in Herzog Chevrolets. Led by crew chief Tony Liberati, a former Winston Cup mechanic and car chief, he made five Busch starts in 1999, with a best finish of seventh.

Johnson's Busch numbers aren't as flashy as others who have advanced to Winston Cup, but he is pleased with his progress. In 2000, he posted six top 10s and finished 10th in points in 31 starts. Last year, he won for the first time, the inaugural Busch race at the new Chicagoland Speedway, logged four top 5s, nine top 10s, and ranked eighth in points after 30 starts.

"If I had been told when I left ASA that I would finish tenth in points the first year in Busch and the second season win a race and finish in the top ten again, I'd have said, 'Shoot, I'll take that,'" Johnson said. "Winning the first race at Chicagoland was awesome. We didn't back into it. We raced hard. We were fortunate to hold off Ryan Newman at the end because he has been incredible in Penske [South] equipment. I am so happy to get the first Busch win for the Herzogs, who have put a lot into me in six years, and for Tony. I feel bad about leaving, but they understand."

Liberati, who remains at Herzog Motor Sports to lead driver Andy Houston this season, believes Johnson is ready for the big league. "He did fine in ASA and Busch," said Liberati, who has worked in Winston Cup seven years. "Tony Stewart didn't win a Busch race, but he set the Winston Cup series on fire as a rookie. Everything is there for Jimmie to be as good as some of the other rookies, to do what Stewart and Harvick did their first year."

From the Desert to Daytona

Johnson didn't get from his 50-cc Suzuki bike at age five to Hendrick Motorsports by himself, as his gratitude to the Herzogs and Liberati attest. He grew up in motorcycle racing, the thing to do in El Cajon at the time, admiring and emulating Rick Johnson (no relation), a seven-time motocross champion. Interestingly enough, Rick Johnson replaced Jimmie as Herzog's ASA driver when Jimmie left for the Busch Series. Jimmie's father, Gary, got him onto motorcycles and—challenged by broken bones and medical bills—off of them into cars and trucks, much to mom Cathy's relief.

Car owner Jeff Bennett gave Johnson his first ride in a race car, a buggy in the Mickey Thompson Stadium Series. That led to his alliance with Fishel and Chevrolet. He honed his driving skills in desert and stadium trucks owned by John Nelson and his father, Pops. In three off-

A Lowe's sponsorship and racing at Lowe's Motor Speedway is a combination guaranteed to get a big hand in driver introductions. *Nigel Kinrade*

In the wake of the September 11 terrorist attacks in 2001, Johnson's Lowe's paint scheme for the season-ending Ford 300 at Homestead-Miami Speedway reflected the surge in patriotic displays. *Nigel Kinrade*

road and stadium series, Johnson won more than 25 races and, including motorcycles, six championships.

With age and experience, Johnson has matured. "I try to race with my brain instead of my feet," he said. "I tore up a lot of off-road equipment because I was young and wide open. I hope I've gotten a lot of that out of my system. I seem to have more control now. There's lots of pressure in Winston Cup, but I think it will be fun."

Johnson's girlfriend, Jessica Bergendahl of Long Beach, California, lends support while he chases his dream. They met at a Christmas party six years ago. Johnson finally got a date with her after nine months of rejection and that led to a "great relationship," Johnson said. "Jessica is a beautiful blonde-haired California girl just like you would imagine. She baby-sits me with genuine support and love. She's never tried to slow me down from what I want to do," he added. "She's working on a master's degree in psychology and has things she wants to do. Someday I'll get married. It's important to have that stability in life."

Away from the track, Johnson, who has a home on Lake Norman—an exclusive Winston Cup bedroom community near Mooresville, North Carolina—enjoys water sports. He spends as much time as his schedule allows with Jessica and his family. His parents have relocated to Mooresville and his dad drives Johnson's motorhome to races. He has two younger brothers, Jarit, 22, and Jesse, 12.

Entering the 2002 season, Jimmie Johnson was an unknown entity to the majority of the Winston Cup garage. At Daytona, Johnson quickly introduced himself by winning the pole for his first Winston Cup race as a regular—the Daytona 500. *Nigel Kinrade*

There's nothing quite like sitting on the pole for the opening laps of the first race of the NASCAR season, especially when that race is the Daytona 500. *Nigel Kinrade*

Johnson's tastes include steak-and-seafood dinners with a glass of wine and alternative rock and country music. He likes to dance, though he is smoother on wheels, he said. He follows the stock market and tries to understand the oft-disturbing news of the world. His TV plays a lot just for the noise.

Johnson has been reading books, some on religion to strengthen his faith, not just because his good friend and fellow driver Blaise Alexander was killed in an Automobile Racing Club of America (ARCA) race at Lowe's Motor Speedway the night of Winston Cup qualifying in October. "It was something I felt inside, and Jessica and I have started growing together," Johnson said. "I think all of us were put here for a reason. It has helped me through the loss of Blaise, another good friend in Wisconsin, and my grandparents. That was hard to grasp, but I'm a lot stronger now. It's made me smile about Blaise instead of being so sad for so long. I think he's in a better place, served his purpose here, and it was time for him to move on."

Above and opposite: It didn't take long for Johnson to find victory lane in Winston Cup. The California native won his first Winston Cup event on April 28, 2002, at California Speedway. *Nigel Kinrade*

Left: The thrill of victory! Johnson needed just nine races to find his way to victory lane in Winston Cup competition, and he did so in front of his hometown fans. *Nigel Kinrade*

Below: Johnson and the rest of the Lowe's crew celebrated with a snapshot at the start/finish line on California's two-mile oval. *Nigel Kinrade*

Jimmie Johnson races up the backstretch at Watkins Glen International, where he had one of the most spectacular crashes in recent history as a Busch Series driver in 2000. Johnson had a brake failure, went off the track, and plowed straight into a huge styrofoam block placed there to help in the event of a crash. He was not hurt. *Nigel Kinrade*

NASCAR's tech inspection area, otherwise known as the "Room of Doom," swallows up the Lowe's Chevrolet during the fall race at Talladega in 2002. *Sam Sharpe*

Continuing his mastery of restrictor-plate tracks, Johnson leads the field to the line from the pole at Talladega. *Nigel Kinrade*

Johnson thought little of a career in NASCAR or Winston Cup until his late teens. He seriously considered Indy cars. As a youth, he was a big fan of three-time Winston Cup champion Cale Yarborough. "Cale was awesome," he said. "He was sponsored by Hardees. When we traveled and stopped at one of the restaurants, I always expected Cale to be there, but he never was." Johnson never met Yarborough, or fallen heroes Davey Allison and Dale Earnhardt. He has met and spent time with another hero, Bobby Allison, over the past two years. "I met a lot of the Winston Cup guys for the first time at my first race."

But meeting Jeff Gordon changed Jimmie Johnson's life, just how much is yet to be determined. And there is no doubt about who is his biggest hero.

For whatever reason, Dover's one-mile concrete oval suited Johnson just fine in 2002. Here he battles with Johnny Benson (10) on his way to victory. *Nigel Kinrade*

Jimmie Johnson was so good at Dover in 2002 that even rival team owners were in his garage asking for help! Jack Roush, who owns five Fords in Winston Cup, chats with Johnson during practice. *Sam Sharpe*

Upon popping out of his car in victory lane, Johnson is either flashing the V for victory sign or he's communicating the number of Winston Cup victories he has in his first full season.
Nigel Kinrade

A TIGHT SQUEEZE

Racing at Bristol is often described as being similar to racing jet planes in a gymnasium because even though the speedway seats around 140,000 fans, its track is a tight fit. Below, Brett Bodine and Terry Labonte trail along in Johnson's wake at the .533-mile high-banked oval. *Nigel Kinrade*

If there's an accident in the works at Bristol, chances are good you'll be involved somehow, as Johnson was in this one. *Nigel Kinrade*

The fast way around Bristol is right on the yellow line around the bottom of the banking, and Johnson is glued to the apron and hard on the gas. *Nigel Kinrade*

Traffic is also a part of racing at Bristol, and Johnson is in the middle of a big wad of cars during the 500-lapper in the spring of 2003. *Nigel Kinrade*

A STOP ON PIT ROAD

The anatomy of a Winston Cup pit stop. In the these photos, the Lowe's crew changes right-side tires and adds fuel. Once finished, the team races around to the left side to perform the same duties. *Sam Sharpe*

ONCE A ROOKIE, NOW A RISING STAR

A Quick Trip to the Top of the Standings

There is a particular script that Jimmie Johnson has followed on his rapid, breathtaking climb from the relatively unknown off-road racing world to the pinnacle of North American motorsports. The script reads: "Start fast, make the most of every opportunity, and keep climbing."

Once his new program with Jeff Gordon and Rick Hendrick had been announced, everyone wondered how many races he would run at the end of the 2001 season to prepare him for his first full Winston Cup season in 2002. His first start came in the UAW-GM Quality 500 at Lowe's Motor Speedway in 2001. He started 15th, a respectable showing for a first-timer, but an accident put him out early and he finished 39th. His next race was at Homestead, and he started 30th and finished 25th. The last race he ran in 2001 saw him finish 29th at Atlanta, three laps down.

After averaging a 31st-place finish in those three races, no one expected much from the team at Daytona in 2002. But, as usual, Johnson made the most of an opportunity. He put his Chevrolet on the pole for the biggest race of the NASCAR season—the Daytona 500—in just his fourth career start.

After the 2002 season, the NASCAR world knew Jimmie Johnson was the real deal. *Nigel Kinrade*

That triumph would lead to four more poles: two at Talladega, the only other track to require the use of restrictor plates, one at Charlotte, and another on the short track at Richmond International Raceway. It also led to victory in his 13th career start, at California, and a sweep of

Top and above: The front row for the Daytona 500 consisted of Johnson and fellow young gun Kevin Harvick. Both drivers would make noise in 2002, with Johnson (right) winning three races and Harvick one. *Nigel Kinrade*

Right: Winning a Gatorade Twin 125 qualifying race at Daytona—especially as a rookie—is quite an accomplishment. *Sam Sharpe*

Winning Winston Cup races is guaranteed to attract the attention of the media. This crush cornered Johnson at the back of his transporter at Dover. *Nigel Kinrade*

No one, not even Jeff Gordon, finished ahead of Johnson at Dover in 2002. He earned a clean sweep of both races at "The Monster Mile." *Nigel Kinrade*

both Dover races. He was the first rookie to ever accomplish that feat. Three victories as a rookie and a fifth-place points finish put him in the same category as the 2002 series champion Tony Stewart, who won three races in his rookie season of 1999 and finished fourth in series points.

Fresh off a rookie season that immediately put him in the upper ranks of Winston Cup drivers, Johnson looked for continued improvement and hoped to avoid the dreaded "sophomore jinx" that has plagued many other young drivers.

Thankfully, for the faithful fans of the No. 48 Lowe's car, he did just that.

—Ron Lemasters Jr.

COOL, CONFIDENT, AND CASHING IN

BY LARRY COTHREN
Stock Car Racing, October 2002

Young Drivers Work Some Marketing Magic and Race All the Way to the Bank

Bill Elliott can look back to his successful run for The Winston Million in 1985 as a time of change during his racing career. The Elliott clan, Bill and brothers Ernie and Dan, claimed R. J. Reynolds' million-dollar bonus that year by winning three of four designated races, but it wasn't simply the money that changed the way the Elliotts operated. Unprecedented attention from the media began to cut deeply into Elliott's time spent working on his car that season. The crush became so bad that Elliott needed armed guards in order to work on his record-setting Thunderbird.

You won't find many Winston Cup drivers today who actually work on their cars, but even more attention is focused on the sport. Instead of preventing drivers from tuning their engines or crawling under their cars to adjust the suspension—as Elliott and a few drivers still did in the mid-1980s—the demands of the sport today might force a driver to be late for a personal appearance, a television interview, or a commercial shoot.

In a world of stock car racing where corporations once feared to tread, marketing terms such as "demographics" and "target audience" are now part of the Sunday afternoon vernacular. And nowhere is marketing

success more prevalent than in the wave of young drivers who have swept to the forefront of NASCAR.

"When we came into this deal, we didn't have any money," Elliott said. "I don't take that as being a negative. I learned what I had to learn during my era. I've been able to adapt throughout the years. I'm very happy today. That's evolution. Guys are going to come in here and push you out. That's part of it. That's the part we've got to understand."

Jimmie Johnson is one young driver who has no problem marketing himself well. *Nigel Kinrade*

Two of the young lions of NASCAR racing do battle at Homestead in the final race of the 2001 season. Dale Earnhardt Jr. (8) battles Johnson during the middle stages of the race. *Nigel Kinrade*

Quick Kids

The current crop of young drivers making waves in the sport—Dale Earnhardt Jr., Elliott Sadler, Kevin Harvick, Kurt Busch, Jimmie Johnson, Ryan Newman, and Casey Atwood, who range in age from 28 to 22 years old—have become familiar to even casual fans of the sport. Over the past decade, a firm foundation for their success has been put in place.

Tony Stewart actually redefined rookie success in 1999 when he won a record three races and finished fourth in Winston Cup points for Joe Gibbs Racing. The trend toward young, successful drivers goes back even further, though, to Jeff Gordon's success as a 22-year-old in 1993, when he was rookie of the year. He won twice the next year and new fans began to flock to the sport because of Gordon. In terms of marketing and appeal to younger, never-before-reached markets, Earnhardt Jr. has picked up where Gordon left off and single-handedly redefined success in the marketplace.

Youthful vigor on the track hasn't equated to positive PR off the track, however. Two of the most successful rookies ever in NASCAR, Stewart and Harvick, have been two of the most volatile drivers off the track. Harvick, who won twice, finished ninth in points and was Cup Rookie of the Year in 2001, has had several well-documented flare-ups this season, as Stewart did in 2001.

This season a young, articulate, well-mannered driver has combined the best of both worlds. Jimmie Johnson is not only saying and doing the right things off the track, he's winning on the track

Johnson has always talked to his fellow drivers. He chats regularly with Dale Earnhardt Jr. (left) and Matt Kenseth (below). *Nigel Kinrade*

at a pace ahead of even Stewart's rookie campaign. By the Pepsi 400 at Daytona, the midpoint of the season, Johnson had won two races and was fourth in points.

Johnson personifies the young, aggressive, winning driver that teams have searched for since Gordon lowered the bar in terms of when to expect success in the sport. For his sponsor, Lowe's, which joined Hendrick Motorsports at the beginning of this season, Johnson's ability to win quickly has meant a reversal of fortunes. The company spent five seasons as a sponsor before reaching

> *"Obviously we've all been given great opportunities and great equipment. A few of us have some great coaches to learn from, so we're all making the most of it."*
>
> —Jimmie Johnson

Going head to head with teammate Jeff Gordon. *Nigel Kinrade*

victory lane in a Winston Cup point race with Richard Childress Racing and driver Robby Gordon in last season's finale at New Hampshire. Lowe's languished in the shadows of NASCAR success while rival Home Depot hit the jackpot in 1999 with Gibbs and Stewart, a combination that produced 12 wins in three seasons.

Getting Noticed

There are parallels between Johnson's success this season and Stewart's in 1999: Both drivers moved to the Winston Cup series after having modest success in the Busch Series, both came from outside

In the first of two annual trips to Pocono, Jimmie earned another pole position. Here, he leads the field to the green flag in front of a huge Pennsylvania crowd. *Nigel Kinrade*

One of the attributes that makes NASCAR racing so unique is the variety of racetracks the series competes on. Here, Johnson battles with Dale Jarrett at the .526-mile Martinsville Speedway in Virginia. *Nigel Kinrade*

the NASCAR realm—Stewart, an Indiana native, came from open-wheel racing, and Johnson, a Californian, came from off-road racing—and both landed with established Winston Cup teams. Their personalities, however, differ as much as the fiery orange and placid blue that make up the primary colors of their respective sponsors.

Home Depot's Hugh Miskel, director of sales development, said Stewart's occasional public relations problems are outweighed by the benefits of exposure gained by the company. "You sort of have the philosophy that if you finish in first or in flames, as long as they're talking about you on Monday morning at the water cooler, you have to view it as a success," Miskel said.

Earning exposure is the name of the game in marketing. When a company is shelling out $10 million or more per year in sponsorship money, getting noticed is of primary concern. Getting noticed in victory lane is the ultimate goal. Companies look for drivers who can perform on the track and behave like gentlemen away from it. Still, young drivers are largely unproven in the major leagues, sometimes with little or no success in a stock car, and even less experience facing a media swarm.

Johnson and Ryan Newman battled until the final race of the 2002 season for Raybestos Rookie of the Year honors. Newman eventually won out. *Sam Sharpe*

"First, you don't know what they can really do in the Cup series, in the top series," said Max Muhleman, president of IMG/Muhleman Marketing. "Then they have their own personal risks. Some of the risks are just like those we see in other major league sports, frankly, where a lot more money than they've ever had before comes their way, and they have 'how-do-they-behave' risks. The other risk, of course, is the one of not being able to do what you expect them to do.

Stewart and Johnson did nothing to set themselves apart in the Busch Series, with Stewart going winless and Johnson winning just once, so both sponsors relied on other mechanisms of

The sweet taste of Victory at Dover (above) was somewhat dulled by the bitter draught of defeat at Daytona. *Sam Sharpe*

evaluation. In aligning with Joe Gibbs Racing and Stewart, Home Depot relied on Gibbs' reputation for success and his ability to deal with people. Lowe's used the same strategy with Hendrick Motorsports and Johnson, relying on Jeff Gordon's assessment of Johnson.

While those two situations paid off quite well, with two of the top seasons ever by Winston Cup rookies, many risks remain in choosing unproven stock car drivers. For every Johnson, there's a Jason Leffler, who dropped back to the NASCAR Craftsman Truck Series this year after spending an unsuccessful 2001 in Winston Cup with Ganassi Racing. For every Stewart, there's a Scott Pruett, a road-racing veteran who was unsuccessful in his attempt to cross over to stock car racing with Cal Wells in 2000.

There's a lot of work that goes into maintaining a Winston Cup car. Johnson's crew, led by Chad Knaus, is one of the best in the business. Knaus (below), son of legendary Chicago-area racer John Knaus, is the perfect match for Johnson.
Nigel Kinrade

Miskel insists that Home Depot's primary motivation to get involved in NASCAR came from the company's employees. The company has used its association with Gibbs and Stewart as a tool to boost morale internally while at the same time giving employees common ground with customers. The impact, buoyed by Stewart's success, has been better than expected.

"I think there is some uncertainty going into any sponsorship as far as what the return is going to be," Miskel said. "The early success of the program exceeded our expectations and has created a very positive umbrella effect over the entire program, which is going to allow it to do more both internally and externally, whether it's [NASCAR] products in our stores or entertainment of customers. And that has and can have a very positive effect on our business overall. I think the outlook for us is very positive because the on-track performance has been a bonus to everything else we've put in place. . . . It has only enhanced everything we've done."

> *"You're always going to have that confrontation between old and young, I guess, and it's a fine balance all the time just getting along with everybody."*
>
> —Kurt Busch

Hendrick Motorsports has always had solid pit crews, and the Lowe's bunch led by Chad Knaus is no exception. This four-tire stop at California contributed to the team's first victory. *Nigel Kinrade*

Bucking Tradition

NASCAR drivers have traditionally been considered in their prime when they reach their mid-30s. So, how can a driver such as a Jimmie Johnson or a Tony Stewart not only win early, but also be consistently competitive, while some of the sport's top names didn't find consistent success until later in their careers? Primarily, the new guys are getting into good equipment quicker than did their predecessors, who had to pay their dues before getting an opportunity in a top car. And with the number of quality sponsors involved today—sponsors who provide the money for successful ventures—there are simply more good cars out there.

Then there's the Gordon factor. Gordon's early success—he was Winston Cup champion soon after turning 24—changed the dynamics of the sport, paving the way for young guys who've followed. With more quality rides available, and with team owners more willing to take a chance on a young driver due to Gordon's success, the result is more young drivers in the limelight.

"Virtually every sponsor is hoping to find the next Jeff Gordon," said Tom Cotter, managing director of CMI Cotter Group, a marketing firm with close ties to the sport. "Because of his success we're seeing a lot more young guys going for it. There are probably a lot of fathers today coaching their kids in go-kart racing and minisprints rather than Little League."

As the Jeff Gordons, Jimmie Johnsons, and Tony Stewarts reach victory lane, NASCAR's fan base expands into new territory. While major league baseball considers contraction and the NBA comes to grips with a future without Michael Jordan, major league stock car racing is reaching an unprecedented number of households, thanks primarily to a billion-dollar television package now in its second year and, yes, thanks to a new wave of young drivers.

Even *Sports Illustrated* took notice earlier this year, putting Dale Earnhardt Jr. on its cover, an undeniably rare placement for a NASCAR driver. With Earnhardt Jr. reaching the pages of *People* magazine and appearing on MTV, and with Gordon making appearances on popular talk shows, NASCAR has become mainstream in America, appealing to a cross-section of fans, especially young ones.

"NASCAR had traditionally appealed to older adults, say from the late twenties, maybe thirty on up," Cotter noted. "But there's a whole huge marketing segment of people who have billions of dollars of marketing power, billions of dollars of buying power that NASCAR has not been at the top of the mind with those people. Having a driver like Jeff Gordon, who appears on the cover of magazines they may read, or more lately Dale Earnhardt Jr., who is appearing on everything that's hip, that's attracting a lot more media

This page and opposite: NASCAR racing is all about horsepower, but there is a commercial aspect to it. Every season, there's a photo shoot for the cars, the drivers, and the crews. At left, Rick Hendrick poses for a team shot with Johnson and Jeff Gordon. *Sam Sharpe*

> *"It's always going to come back to who can win.*
> *The guy who's got five or ten years, but not twenty, under his belt and has got real talent and a good team is always going to be dominant."*
>
> —Max Muhleman,
> motorsports marketing executive

Fans are an important part of every NASCAR driver's duties. Jimmie has been one of the best in the garage at signing everything he can. Because of his willingness to sign autographs, he sometimes gets mobbed, as he did above at Michigan Speedway in 2003. *Top photo: Nigel Kinrade, Above photo: Sam Sharpe*

attention in the media of a particular demographic type. It's hard to escape NASCAR. That's how you breed new blood to take over the reins of fandom in this sport."

As the fan base grows, the sport benefits in several ways. "The interesting thing is both of the cola companies are in it and they have one of the youngest demo skews of anybody," Muhleman said. "They're interested in demographics down to twelve years old, which is a lot younger than motor oil or something like that. As the demographics improve, the sponsor net gets wider."

The End Result

Sponsors, meanwhile, have become increasingly impatient in recent seasons, as the demand to win correlates directly with the amount of money spent. "Silly Season," NASCAR's annual period of driver changes and rumors of driver changes, experienced a spring renewal this year, earlier than ever before, primarily because of impatient sponsors and the pressures team owners face.

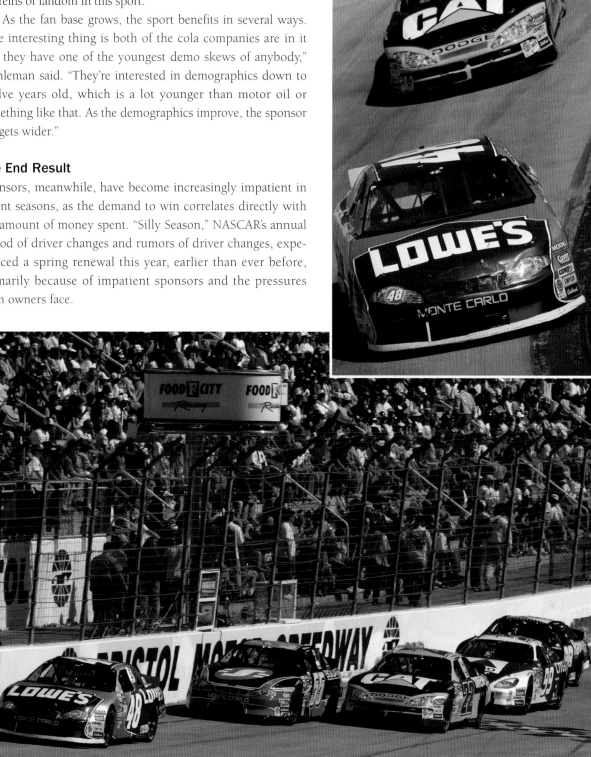

Racing close together is part and parcel of racing at Bristol, as Johnson, Bobby Hamilton (55), Ward Burton (22), Jeff Burton (99), and Ricky Rudd (28) demonstrate in 2002's spring race. Ward Burton (top) couldn't handle Johnson at Bristol. *Nigel Kinrade*

The pits at Bristol Motor Speedway are a busy place as Jimmie Johnson pulls in for service. *Nigel Kinrade*

"There seems to be a lot more immediacy now," Cotter said. "The price of sponsorship has gone up so dramatically in recent years [that] there is not as much patience to wait for a program to come around and start showing benefits and increasing sales of whatever product a company has.

"There used to be, 'Plant the seed and we'll wait for sales to rise.' Now it's much more immediate: 'We want to start seeing increased sales over the next two quarters,' and there has to be measurement mechanisms put in place. The reason for that is racing has gotten expensive. It's on the radar charts now, not as just throwing away a couple of million dollars and saying, 'We'll see what happens.'"

It remains to be seen whether the current youth movement will be a lasting trend or a passing phenomenon, whether 20-something drivers will be leading the sport or merely following experienced veterans. In every other major sport, after all, athletes typically are most productive before age 35. Should stock car racing be any different?

Of the 19 different winners last season [2002], five were 30 or younger, and five of 11 winners were 31 or younger during the first half of this season. Second-year driver Kurt Busch was 23 when he won at Bristol during March of this year, joining Johnson, who was 26 when he won at

Veteran Sterling
Marlin chases
Johnson through
the flat turn three
at Pocono Raceway.
Nigel Kinrade

California, his first Cup victory. Six winners last year [2002] were over 40, however, and five were 40 or older during this season's first 17 races.

"Obviously, we've all been given great opportunities and great equipment," Johnson said. "A few of us have some great coaches to learn from, so we're all making the most of it. Don't be fooled. The veterans, they're on their game; they're up front battling and winning as well."

The driver leading the point race during much of the first half of the 2002 season was 45-year-old Sterling Marlin, a veteran in his 17th full season of competition. The point race by midseason produced an even mix of drivers in the top 10—five were over 40 and five were 31 or younger, including relative youngsters Gordon, Johnson, Stewart, Kenseth, and Busch.

Busch compares it to being a high school student, which he was just six years ago. "You're always going to have the elder statesmen and the younger statesmen," he said. "It's similar to high school where you've got freshmen coming in [and] they think they know everything; they're going to get on the varsity football team and do their own deal. Then, of course, you've got the veterans there

Casey Mears and John Andretti chase after the competitive Johnson at Rockingham in 2002. *Nigel Kinrade*

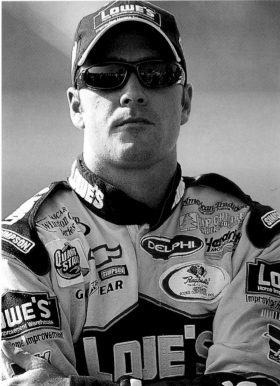

Johnson is a fierce competitor, and he spends a lot of time thinking his way through the problems he faces each week. *Nigel Kinrade*

Jimmie Johnson always races well in his home state of California. Above, he tackles the road course at Infineon Raceway near San Francisco. Right, he contemplates his strategy in the garage area at California Speedway. *Nigel Kinrade*

HOW THEY COMPARE

Are today's youngsters reaching victory lane at an age younger than drivers from the past? A glance at the top six drivers on NASCAR Winston Cup's all-time win list compared with five of today's young drivers shows both groups winning at the same approximate age.

Richard Petty, number one on the win list, was 22 when he claimed his initial win. David Pearson was 26; Bobby Allison was 28; Darrell Waltrip was 28; Cale Yarborough was 25; and Dale Earnhardt was 27 (28 days before his 28th birthday).

The average age of the top six all-time winners when they first won in Winston Cup? Twenty-six. The average age of Kurt Busch, Dale Earnhardt Jr., Kevin Harvick, Jimmie Johnson, and Elliott Sadler when each won his first race? Twenty-five.

Jeff Gordon, seventh in all-time wins, was 22, same as Petty, when he won his first race, and he was the Winston Cup champion at 24. Tony Stewart was 28 when he first won a Winston Cup race in 1999, and Matt Kenseth was 28 when he notched his first win in 2000. In 1987, Davey Allison was 26 when he won two races, becoming the first rookie since Earnhardt in 1979 to score a win.

If the past is any indication, today's young drivers have a lot to look forward to when they reach their 30s. Petty won 129 races from age 29 to 38, and Waltrip won all three of his driving titles between the ages of 34 and 38.

All of the drivers on the all-time win list, in fact, enjoyed the bulk of their success in their mid-30s, with the exception of Pearson, who put together one of his best seasons in 1976, at the age of 41, and Allison, who won his only Winston Cup title at age 45 in 1983.

Yarborough won consecutive championships in 1976, 1977, and 1978, when he was between the ages of 36 and 38. Earnhardt was still winning races at age 49, but the bulk of his success came between the ages of 34 and 44, and he turned 36 the year he won a career-high 11 races in 1987.

who know how things are and they're going to put them in their place. You're always going to have that confrontation between old and young, I guess, and it's a fine balance all the time just getting along with everybody."

Muhleman sees the sport going through a normal transition and not a profound, landscape-altering trend toward younger drivers, as Marlin, Dale Jarrett, Rusty Wallace, Terry Labonte, and other over-40 drivers near the end of their careers.

"It's always going to come back to who can win," Muhleman said. "The guy who's got five or ten years, but not twenty, under his belt and has got real talent and a good team is always going to be dominant. They're going to win with all things being anywhere near equal.

"It's a cycle, really, that sometimes has not been as obvious as other times. Right now it's a very obvious thing. These guys are going to get old. In five years, they'll be five years older. I don't mean to be facetious, but Jeff Gordon is thirty and he's not included with the young guys anymore. I mean, it seems like yesterday [Dale] Earnhardt and everybody was calling him 'Wonder Boy,' and now, while he's not 'Pops' yet, he's not ever mentioned as a younger driver. Isn't that amazing?"

PEOPLE'S CHOICE AWARDS' BIGGEST SURPRISE IN 2002:

Stock Car Racing, November 2002

Jimmie Johnson

Sure his car owner is Jeff Gordon, sure he's got the best equipment, but the 2002 season was supposed to be more of a learning curve for Jimmie Johnson. Instead, this guy goes out and quite often spanks most of the field. Go figure.

First of all, Johnson rolls out at Daytona and lands the pole for the 500. OK, just a fluke, right? After all, this former off-road racer hadn't exactly lit up the field in the NASCAR Busch Series, leaving with just one win.

The foundation of Hendrick Motorsports at Daytona in 2002: Team owner Rick Hendrick (far left) stands with drivers Terry Labonte, Jeff Gordon, and Jimmie Johnson. *Nigel Kinrade*

Being on the same page, as Johnson and Knaus are, often means being in victory lane at the end of the day. *Sam Sharpe*

Poles are an important part of winning in NASCAR, and Johnson certainly has a sense of timing. Here he celebrates winning the pole for the Coca-Cola 600 at Lowe's Motor Speedway with Chad Knaus (left) and team owner Rick Hendrick. *Sam Sharpe*

There's a look in the eyes of a champion, and Jimmie Johnson has it. *Nigel Kinrade*

A trip around the track is part of the process for driver introductions. Here, Johnson waits his turn. *Sam Sharpe*

But by the midseason of 2002, Johnson had reached Winston Cup's victory lane not once, but twice. He rested comfortably in third place in the point standings, a stone's throw from first and ahead of his boss. Hey Jimmie, didn't anyone ever tell you it's not cool to beat the boss?!

Some have already hailed him as the best rookie in memory. Then again, it wasn't too awful long ago that Tony Stewart and Kevin Harvick were standing the racing world on its ear as a rookie. Now it's Johnson who may set the standard for how rookies will be judged in the future.

Johnson's confidence grows with each new race, and that's enough to keep even the wily veterans on edge. Some may argue that this fellow will only be another flash in the pan in racing history, but more likely we're witnessing the birth of the sport's next superstar.

TRULY A TEAM EFFORT

Behind the scenes, many people have a hand in making a race team successful. Here, members of Jimmie Johnson's team put the final touches on the Lowe's Chevrolet on race day. *Sam Sharpe*

Every one of these teams needs a leader, and in Jimmie Johnson's case, that leader is crew chief Chad Knaus. *Sam Sharpe*

Ryan McCray is the front tire carrier for the team, so for every race he's out there on pit road with cars whizzing past only inches away. *Sam Sharpe*

Jim Pollard handles the gas cans for the pit stop crew. *Sam Sharpe*

Kansas Speedway was a real pit of vipers for Johnson in 2003. After winning the pole, he crashed his primary car and had to go to a backup for the race. *Nigel Kinrade*

Other drivers can often help troubleshoot a crash. Here, Johnson runs it by Dale Earnhardt Jr. following his crash at Kansas. *Nigel Kinrade*

Starting last in a
43-car field is bad
enough, but knowing
you should be starting
first makes it that
much worse. That's
what Johnson had to
think about after
crashing his pole-
winning car in practice.
Nigel Kinrade

It was a long day at Kansas, but Johnson drove through the field to earn another top finish. *Nigel Kinrade*

A MILLION-DOLLAR EFFORT

Johnson crosses the finish line first at the final running of The Winston all-star race at Lowe's Motor Speedway, thus earning a cool $1 million. *Sam Sharpe*

One of the pleasures of winning these days is the post-race burnout. Here, Johnson lights the tires in front of the Lowe's sign after winning The Winston. *Sam Sharpe*

This was Johnson's first victory in the race for event winners, and it foreshadowed his success a week later in the Coca-Cola 600. *Nigel Kinrade*

STRIVING TO BE NUMBER ONE

Just When Will Johnson Win It All?

Following a rookie season that saw him win three races, Jimmie Johnson entered 2003 as one of a handful of favorites to win the last NASCAR Winston Cup title. *Sam Sharpe*

After his 2002 rookie season in NASCAR's Winston Cup division, it is hard to imagine that Jimmie Johnson could do even better one year later. And while he had a rough beginning of the season, he finished the year stronger than ever.

"It was just a great year for the entire Lowe's team," Johnson said following the season-ending race at the new Homestead-Miami Speedway. "I never in my wildest dreams expected to have six victories [for his career], The Winston, all the poles, and a fifth-place [points] finish last year, and a second-place finish this year. But we're here. I'm just getting all I can every day, every lap and so are Chad [Knaus, crew chief] and the entire team. We have a great relationship, great equipment, and great sponsors. You hear everybody saying that stuff, but it really is the truth. Our sport is about people. The top teams all have the same equipment. It's all about people. I'm so fortunate to have the crew that I do. They've made a sophomore finish second this year."

For the record, Johnson won both races at New Hampshire International Speedway as well as the rain-shortened Coca-Cola 600 at Lowe's Motor Speedway. A week before his victory at the track whose naming rights are owned by his sponsor, Lowe's Home Improvement Warehouse, Johnson won the final running of The Winston all-star event at the same speedway—and more than $1 million of Winston's money. (The 2004 event will be held at Lowe's, but it is sponsored by Nextel.)

His first triumph of 2003 at New Hampshire in July gave Chevrolet its 400th victory of NASCAR's modern era, which began in 1972 when the schedule was trimmed from 48 races to 31. His second, in September, came after seeing three members of his pit crew hit on pit road by his team owner and teammate Jeff Gordon during the first caution of the race.

Johnson and his pit crew, ready to tackle their second season in the Winston Cup. *Sam Sharpe*

This duel, during the annual Coca-Cola 600 at Lowe's Motor Speedway, featured the top two finishers in the 2003 NASCAR Winston Cup point standings. Matt Kenseth (17) trails Johnson, as Dave Blaney (77) moves to the inside. *Nigel Kinrade*

Since Lowe's holds the naming rights to the former Charlotte Motor Speedway, Johnson's Lowe's Chevy often sports a new paint scheme for the annual Coca-Cola 600. Here's the 2002 version. *Nigel Kinrade*

Jeff Gordon (left) is no slouch at getting around Lowe's Motor Speedway, but his protégé was the man to beat in May, winning both The Winston and the Coca-Cola 600. *Nigel Kinrade*

There's nothing better than winning a race at your sponsor's racetrack, especially when it completes a two-week sweep worth $2 million in prize money. Johnson had to hoist his Coca-Cola 600 trophy inside the garage area after a rain shower ended the race early. *Nigel Kinrade*

"It's weird," Johnson said of his two season sweeps. "We were able to do it at Dover last year and then again this year at New Hampshire. Coming in [after winning there in July], there's a lot of pressure on you to do this. We had the same race car, the same things, we were good in practice. We knew all the ingredients were there. You sleep on it all night long and wonder how you're going to mess it up. It's really tough to do. Today, with what happened on pit road, I thought, 'We're just going to have to salvage what we can.' Chad [crew chief Chad Knaus] came on the radio and said, 'Hey, bud, you're 16th now and we need a top ten. We need good points, let's just get good points.'

"I was under the same realization that it was going to be virtually impossible for us to get to the front, but once everybody got strung out and we started passing guys, before we knew it we were in second. So it was meant to be. It's very hard to come back and repeat, and I'm glad that we've done it. We're the first ones to do it in the eighteen years they've been coming here. It's a huge honor, but a huge amount of stress for the last week knowing that New Hampshire was the next one all the way through taking the checkered flag."

Finding time to laugh during the long Winston Cup season is essential to good mental health. Jimmie had plenty of reasons to smile in 2003. *Nigel Kinrade*

After winning the two races at Lowe's Motor Speedway in May, Johnson was the odds-on favorite during the first night running of the UAW-GM Quality 500, but he did not earn a second season sweep. Tony Stewart won the event. *Nigel Kinrade*

In 2002, Johnson won both races at Dover Downs International Speedway in Delaware, giving him a season sweep in each of his first two seasons in Winston Cup racing. He also won at his home track, California Speedway, in April, making him the toast of the coast for a different reason.

Some of NASCAR's "young guns" have been impressive in flashes, winning spectacularly one week and finishing out of the running the next. Johnson's main challenger for Rookie of the Year honors in 2002, Ryan Newman, is a prime example of this. Despite a series-best eight victories in 2003, Newman was fourth in the points based on several DNFs throughout the season. Johnson, on the other hand, has been in the top 10 in NASCAR points for the past 70 races, the best current streak and ninth all-time in the modern era. The late Dale Earnhardt, a seven-time Winston Cup champion, holds the all-time mark at 161.

Johnson's consistency—14 top-5 and 20 top-10 finishes in 36 races—paid off when it counted late in the season

After sweeping both races at Dover in his rookie season, Johnson was looking to make it three straight on the Delaware track in June. However, a lap-277 crash put him out for the day and dropped him to 38th at the finish. Before his crash, Johnson was among the best cars on the track at Dover. He led 36 laps, most of them with team owner and teammate Jeff Gordon on his back bumper. *Nigel Kinrade*

It used to be that Jimmie Johnson went to other drivers for advice. Now, other drivers, such as Elliott Sadler, come to him. *Nigel Kinrade*

A rematch of the 2002 Raybestos Rookie of the Year battle between Ryan Newman (12) and Jimmie Johnson at Darlington during the final Labor Day running of the Southern 500. *Sam Sharpe*

as he chased runaway point leader Matt Kenseth for the title. Although Kenseth clinched the title with one race remaining, Johnson waged a hot and heavy battle for second with Dale Earnhardt Jr., Jeff Gordon, and Ryan Newman. Kenseth blew an engine in the final race at Homestead, finishing 43rd, and Johnson soldiered home third, making Kenseth's final margin just 90 points.

"Maybe in the last few years, the speed has been with these younger drivers but maybe not the consistency," Johnson said. "Everybody out there is a very smart race car driver in learning the dos and don'ts and how to be consistent and not get into wrecks and have problems. I think the young faces you see will continue to be there. But at the same time it's not about age—look at [46-year-old] Bill Elliott. He's been strong for the last three months [of 2003]. It's about communication and it's about people."

In finishing second to Kenseth, Johnson regards his team's performance as the harbinger of even more success in 2004. "Being the first loser doesn't bother me too

In the thick of the championship chase, communication between driver and crew chief is critical. Johnson and crew chief Chad Knaus weathered the storm of the championship battle, talking strategy at Atlanta Motor Speedway at the end of the season. *Nigel Kinrade*

Chad Knaus and Jimmie Johnson compare notes following practice at Martinsville. *Sam Sharpe*

Hard on the gas at Atlanta, Johnson leads the way. *Sam Sharpe*

Martinsville is the
shortest track on
the Winston Cup
series at .526 miles
and a tough place
to race, especially
when the next race
on the schedule
is at Talladega
Superspeedway,
the longest track the
series visits at 2.66
miles. *Nigel Kinrade*

Here, Johnson runs amid a gaggle on the .526-mile Martinsville oval. *Sam Sharpe*

much," Johnson quipped. "I didn't expect to be in this position. Of course I wanted to win the championship [in 2003]. I wanted to win it [in 2002] and do something that no one's ever done. It doesn't mean that we're not putting in everything that we can. But we're in a position where we don't need to put any additional pressure on ourselves. If you look at history, it usually takes three, four, or five years to get the driver and the team into championship form. Maybe next year will be that special year for us. It takes a lot of luck. If you look at Matt Kenseth's year, he's been fast and done all the right things, but he's had flat tires at the right point in time and only been caught up in one or two wrecks and blown one engine. That's hard to do. We'll give it one hundred percent [in 2004] and see what happens."

For his part, Johnson had a few miscues himself during the season. At Talladega, Johnson was running for the lead with the Dale Earnhardt Inc. duo of Michael Waltrip and Earnhardt Jr. when the latter made contact with Waltrip, shoving Waltrip into Johnson and sending him sliding through turn one. He recovered from that setback and was in position to claim a top-5 finish when the engine blew. He finished 34th.

As Johnson gets ready to go to war at Talladega, one member of the Army's elite Black Knight parachute team floats (in upper right hand corner) down toward the speedway. *Sam Sharpe*

Racing in a pack is the order of the day at Talladega, and Johnson is right in the thick of it.
Nigel Kinrad

Johnson is the meat in a three-wide sandwich during the fall race at Talladega, and Casey Mears (41) and Robby Gordon are the bread. Kenny Wallace (23) and Ryan Newman (12) trail the action.
Sam Sharpe

Jimmie Johnson straps into his car before the 2003 Chevy Monte Carlo 400 at Richmond. *Sam Sharpe*

A modern-day mechanized warrior, Johnson is surrounded by the latest in motorsports safety equipment. Note that Johnson wears the HANS (head and neck safety) device rather than the Hutchens Device. *Nigel Kinrade*

He ran out of gas at Michigan and crashed at Dover, but consistency overcame the occasional error every time. "You look across the board and there are a lot of those out there," he said. "At the end of the year, the guy with the shortest list of 'what ifs' will be the champion. The competition is too close. Everybody is going to win. Everybody is going to win poles. Everybody is going to be up front. It's that 'what if' category at the end of the year."

Johnson gives much credit to car owners Rick Hendrick and Jeff Gordon and to Knaus and to the members of his team. Despite the fact that he's a relative youngster, at least in terms of time in NASCAR's premier series, Johnson is a keen observer of the sport and all that goes into it. Consider his remarks on long-time sponsor R. J. Reynolds and its Winston brand, which ended a 33-year run as series sponsor in 2003.

In the first of many trips to victory lane in his career, Johnson shares the spotlight with Miss Winston following his first career victory in 2002 at California Speedway. *Nigel Kinrade*

One race Johnson has never won is the Brickyard 400. It's one he wants to win. *Nigel Kinrade*

Johnson has always run well at Darlington, which is perhaps the toughest track on the NASCAR circuit. Here, he gets service from his crew at the legendary "Track Too Tough to Tame." *Nigel Kinrade*

Tires flying, the Lowe's crew hustles to get Johnson out ahead of the pack at Darlington. *Nigel Kinrade*

A Winston Cup pit crew can change four tires, fill the car full of fuel, make adjustments, and clean the windshield in a shade under 14 seconds. *Nigel Kinrade*

"With only having two years in the Winston Cup series, I've gotten to know the faces, but I haven't really been able to see what they've done," Johnson said of Winston. "When they entered the sport, I was just a twinkle in my mom and dad's eyes. I wasn't even here [he laughs]. But I can say that I've wanted to race in Winston Cup all my life. Good or bad, I didn't realize that it was a cigarette brand. I thought it was just what NASCAR called it. That's all that I've ever known. That's what I've wanted to do, and it's more popular than ever now. But they've done a lot for the sport and some of the veterans can speak better to that than I can. I'm thankful for everything that they've done."

Following his first two seasons in NASCAR's top division, it stands to reason that many are going to be thankful that Jimmie Johnson will be part of their sport for years to come.

—Ron Lemasters Jr.

As part of his late-season run toward the title, Johnson placed fifth in the final Labor Day running of the Southern 500 at Darlington. After the race, he trailed eventual Winston Cup champion Matt Kenseth by 485 points; he lost the title to Kenseth by a mere 90. *Nigel Kinrade*

This is a view that most competitors have come to dread: It means Jimmie Johnson is hot on your tail. *Sam Sharpe*

THE *STOCK CAR* INTERVIEW

Jimmie Johnson

BY JASON MITCHELL
Stock Car Racing, September 2003

Editor's note: Coming off a stellar rookie season, many people pegged Jimmie Johnson as a championship contender for 2003. But the driver from California has learned quickly how tough it can be to repeat success. He brushes aside any notions of a "sophomore jinx" and chooses instead to learn from the tough, inevitable lessons. Johnson recently discussed his road to Winston Cup stardom with Stock Car Racing.

It's a safe bet to say the results you pulled off last year were something that seemed like a dream. At what point in time did all that success sink in?

I would say during the winter it started to sink in and I was able to realize what an amazing season we had. To accomplish the things we did with a rookie team was great. I really haven't had the time to sit down and reflect on it all that much. I'm always on the go and always thinking about the next week, so I haven't really let it sink in. My mom and the rest of my family have kept the articles and pictures, so I'm sure one day I'll sit down with my kids or grandkids and tell them stories of me in Winston Cup racing.

How have you managed to handle all the success that you've experienced so quickly?

I really didn't have much of a choice. Kevin Harvick called me after I won my first race and told me how my life would never be the same, and he was totally right. There is nothing that you can do to prepare yourself for what comes when you start racing Winston Cup and start having success. You get pulled in so many directions and stretched so thin that you have to put the right people in place and create some structure around the madness or it will just eat you up and drive you crazy. This is an area that Jeff Gordon has helped me out in, and we have created a schedule that allows me to have some time for myself and fulfill all of the things I need and want to do.

What was the high point of last season for you? Was it that first Winston Cup victory or the fact that you backed it up with two more wins and ended up fifth in the final point standings?

I would say backing it up with two victories and finishing in the top five overall at the end of the year. The first win was incredible, but it was a new experience and it was like rush here, rush there. I didn't get a chance to savor the moment because I didn't know what to expect. With the wins at Dover, on the other hand, I

This is the face of a million-dollar man on the evening of The Winston at Lowe's in 2003. *Sam Sharpe*

Chevrolet had a spectacular season in 2003, winning 19 races and the manufacturer's championship. Johnson won three of those 19 races, and Robby Gordon (31) won both the events on road courses. *Nigel Kinrade*

The title contenders do battle at Dover. Matt Kenseth (17) races alongside Johnson. *Sam Sharpe*

Friends off the track, Johnson and Matt Kenseth hang out in the garage between practice sessions. *Nigel Kinrade*

Johnson leads Ryan Newman, who led the series with eight victories in 2003. *Nigel Kinrade*

knew what was coming and I appreciated them more. And to finish fifth overall is something that very few people thought we could do at the start of the season. I had a great time at the banquet in New York and hopefully we will be going back there for many years to come.

Your performance left many people expecting you to win a championship soon. Is the team at that level?

This team has all of the ingredients to contend for the championship. We have the support from Hendrick Motorsports and Lowe's, plus we have kept this team intact. These guys, including [crew chief] Chad [Knaus] and I, know what it takes to be a championship contender. We know how much effort and dedication it will take and we are continuing to grow as a team and support each other week in and week out. If we can just cut out the peaks and valleys in our finishes and just remain consistent each week, we'll be championship contenders for a long time to come.

How much more comfortable have you been in your second season of Winston Cup racing compared to your first go-around?

Going to the tracks the second time, being in the garage, and knowing faces and routines and everything that's going on have made things a lot more comfortable. After the year we had last year, the confidence that I've gotten has been tremendous. It's been a huge thing for me and has really made my second year a lot more enjoyable.

This is pretty much how Jimmie Johnson's 2003 season went—a big thumbs-up after finishing second in the points. *Sam Sharpe*

How concerned were you about experiencing a "sophomore jinx" in 2003?

I don't have that fear. Every racer has pressure to perform, whether you're a four-time Winston Cup champion or a rookie team trying to make a race. You will always have pressure to perform. The only thing that we can do is to be prepared each week and give 100 percent each week. If we do that, I'm confident that the rest will take care of itself.

When you were in contention for the championship last year, you said that if you didn't win the title that it would be OK because you would have more opportunities later in your

Being a Winston Cup driver is all about focus, and Jimmie Johnson is certainly focused here. *Nigel Kinrade*

Michigan is a fast, wide-open racetrack, and Johnson takes advantage of the high line around the tri-oval. *Nigel Kinrade*

career. But after getting off to somewhat of a slow start in 2003 before picking up the back-to-back victories in The Winston and the Coca-Cola 600, do you think opportunities to win the title come around only once or twice in a lifetime?

I do have a better understanding of the difficulties in competing and winning races and winning championships. It's very hard. Last year, when I made that comment, I felt we'd have another opportunity. With our being a rookie team last year, the worst thing we could do was to have that pressure on our shoulders. We were putting ourselves in that position by not thinking or worrying about that. As soon as that pressure starts to creep in, then you change. That's what we were trying to avoid this year. With the future at hand, who knows when that opportunity will happen again? I think Mark Martin has finally realized that, and we all know how hard he's been on himself for years and years about not getting a championship. You can't deny the man the effort and dedication he's put into it, but it just hasn't happened for him yet. I don't want to find myself or my team in that situation.

This is the most important part of the car when it comes to downforce. The nose, new for the Chevrolet Monte Carlo in 2003, helps keep air on the front of the car, which pushes down on the front wheels and helps the driver turn the car. *Nigel Kinrade*

Johnson has always been a factor on restrictor-place tracks, despite the fact he has never won a restrictor-plate race. Here he battles with another young star, Kurt Busch, during the Daytona 500. *Nigel Kinrade*

Right: Hendrick Motorsports is all about teamwork. Here, Hendrick Motorsports engine guru Randy Dorton (left) takes the time to discuss options with both Jimmie Johnson and Jeff Gordon. *Nigel Kinrade*

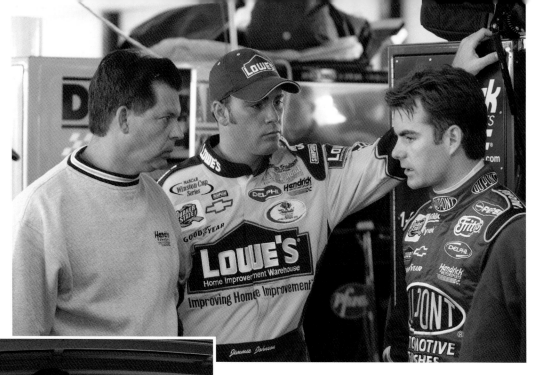

Left: Johnson further discusses a setup with Chad Knaus and a crew member.

Below: Jeff Gordon (right) and Jimmie Johnson share a moment on pit lane at Rockingham, bundled up against the February cold. *Sam Sharpe*

Johnson leads Jeff Gordon onto pit road at New Hampshire on his way to a second straight victory there in 2003. Earlier, as the cars came down pit road the first time, Gordon ran into three of Johnson's crew members and knocked them down. All three were shaken but finished their duties and missed no action. A late-race stop put Johnson in position to win. *Nigel Kinrade*

Celebrating his second sweep in as many seasons, Johnson salutes the fans at New Hampshire International Speedway. *Nigel Kinrade*

Jeff Gordon (24) earned a season sweep of his own at Martinsville in 2003. Here, he drives to the inside of his protégé/ teammate Johnson off turn four.
Sam Sharpe

There have been times when Jeff Gordon and his team have really seemed to be relying on you and crew chief Chad Knaus for setup information. What is it like being a sophomore driver trying to give advice to a four-time Winston Cup champion?

The No. 24 and No. 48 teams share a shop and work together very closely. Really, all four of the Hendrick Motorsports teams work together and rely on each other for information and help. With the way that NASCAR has limited the number of tests that teams have this season, sharing information is even more important now then it has been in the past. It's great that the No. 24 team and the other Hendrick teams feel comfortable with us and can use our information to help them. It really is a family philosophy at Hendrick.

It seemed like Jeff Gordon really became receptive to some of the new attitudes and approaches that have been working for you. Do you agree that you helped him like he has said on countless occasions?

I feel like Chad Knaus is responsible for that. He has brought in new, fresh ideas, and with the way the sport is changing and evolving, Chad is really aggressive in trying some unique setups. Without me being in the sport for a long time and not having strong feelings to a certain setup on certain tracks, I've been really open-minded. The setups Chad has brought to me have helped me with my driving style. In a roundabout way, I think that's what Jeff Gordon is talking about. These cars are ever-changing, and the way you drive them changes with each setup change. I'm able to get a handle with the new setups we're running and learn them relatively quickly because I don't have any past experience. I've been able to teach Jeff a little about that, too.

As part of a summer promotion, Johnson's team bore the colors of the popular Nickelodeon cartoon series *SpongeBob SquarePants*. Here, Johnson and Sponge Bob get acquainted on the pit lane at Daytona. *Nigel Kinrade*

Johnson started second at Pocono in July, but fell victim to polesitter Ryan Newman's powerful Alltel Dodge. *Nigel Kinrade*

Powering around the flat third turn at Pocono, Johnson runs away from Elliott Sadler. *Nigel Kinrade*

Champagne is a big part of victory lane celebrations, and Jimmie got all he could out of this magnum at Charlotte. *Sam Sharpe*

Gatorade is a big part, too, and Johnson sprays the crowd following his first victory at New Hampshire International Speedway in July. The victory was Chevrolet's 400th of the modern era. *Sam Sharpe*

Some people in the media have made it a point this year to talk about whether Jeff Gordon has been somewhat bewildered that you have come along and had an immediate impact. What are your thoughts on that subject?

I don't think that has Jeff miffed or that he thinks I'm even upstaging him. He's a competitor and I'm a competitor. If you'll notice, during the race when it's time for give and take, both of us play that game pretty well together and give each other the breaks that are needed. When you get to the end of the race and have a million dollars on the line like we did at The Winston, both of us are going at each other as hard as we do anyone else. Would I turn Jeff around to have a position or would I rough him up? No. That's my teammate and I wouldn't do that to any of my teammates, but I'm going to race him as hard as I can.

You've taken the path not normally traveled to reach the Winston Cup level after a great deal of success in off-road racing, with six championships. Because you did have limited Busch Series experience, how much of a surprise was it to you when you were approached about the idea of starting a fourth Winston Cup team at Hendrick Motorsports?

I was a little taken aback when I spoke with Jeff about the idea. I really haven't spent much more than two years in each series that I've raced in. After two years, I move on. Thankfully, Jeff and Rick [Hendrick] saw something in me, and I've been able to take the tools that they've supplied us with and have had success with them. It's a great feeling being associated with one of the premier organizations in all of motorsports.

Was there any hesitation in the fact you might have taken on more than you could handle?

No. The plan for the No. 48 Lowe's team is for the future. We are all relatively young guys on this team, and we are still learning and growing. It just happened that the fit was perfect, and we had success right from the start. However, this team was built for the future, and we'll only get better with time and experience.

On the other side of that, how personally satisfying has it been for you to not only race but also beat veteran and champion drivers on a regular basis in making a name for yourself?

It's weird to be racing alongside of guys and beating guys that were my idols growing up. Last season in Darlington, I was coming off pit road with the No. 88 behind me, and we all know how good Dale Jarrett is at Darlington. We got going and I just thought to myself, "Here we go, because D. J. is going to eat me up." Three laps into that run, I looked in my rearview mirror and I was pulling away from him. I was amazed, and I think that was one instance when I started building some confidence in the fact that I could run with guys like Jeff Gordon, Mark Martin, and Dale Jarrett on a regular basis.

Since 1950, the Southern 500 has run on Labor Day weekend at Darlington Raceway. The raced moved to November in 2004, making the 2003 running a very special event. Hendrick Motorsports teammate Terry Labonte won the 2003 race. *Nigel Kinrade*

Jimmie Johnson races into turn one at the Indianapolis Motor Speedway during the Brickyard 400. Indianapolis is perhaps the best-known motorsports facility on the planet. *Sam Sharpe*

How much of a job has it been trying to satisfy everybody from the media to all the folks who pay the bills?

It's a full-time job being a driver. You just have to create a structure or routine that allows you to take care of everything. Mondays are my days off. Tuesdays, I have a media conference call. Wednesdays, I do laundry, pay bills, etc., and do media or sponsor activities if necessary. Thursdays, I travel to the races. Then, we are into the race weekend and that is filled with racing, sponsor activities, charity events, etc. You really have to make time for things because if you don't, it will never happen.

Out to the grid at Indianapolis, through the throng, and under the famed Gasoline Alley arch. *Sam Sharpe*

Getting his game face on, Jimmie Johnson prepares to do battle one more time. *Sam Sharpe*

Johnson flips the switches to bring his Lowe's Chevrolet to life prior to the spring race at Martinsville in 2003. *Sam Sharpe*

How much time do you get to spend with your family now that you're a busy Winston Cup superstar?

I'm not sure about the superstar tag there, but it's very challenging to spend time with them. Shortly after I started racing in the Busch Series, my family moved from California to North Carolina. My father drives my motor coach to virtually every race and my mom works on my fan club. So they are still very much involved in my life. My little brother, Jesse, drives a Bandolero, and my other brother, Jarit, is his crew chief and spends a lot of time building and fine-tuning the car. Jesse races Tuesday nights at Lowe's Motor Speedway, so when I'm in town on a Tuesday, it's a safe bet that I'll be there supporting both of them and helping out in any way possible. Besides that, we all live about five miles away from each other, so we try and get together as much as possible.

What is one thing most race fans don't know about Jimmie Johnson that they might find interesting?

People would be surprised to know that I'm just an average person who has a really cool job. I still do laundry, pay bills, wash dishes, do yard work—all the same things that everyone else has to do. Many people think that as drivers, we have people that do all of the things, but many of us don't. We're just the average next-door neighbors.

A couple of stars race hard under the moon. Jimmie Johnson and Tony Stewart (20) do battle at Richmond. *Sam Sharpe*

Television has a big influence on today's NASCAR drivers. Here, Johnson talks with ESPN's Mike Massaro in the garage area.
Sam Sharpe

Here Johnson waves to a crowd of fans and members of the press early on in his Cup career—at the 2002 Daytona Speedweeks. *Nigel Kinrade*

DRIVER RANKINGS 2004

BY LARRY COTHREN

Stock Car Racing, March 2004

How the Inaugural Nextel Cup Points Battle Will Unfold

Jimmie Johnson has his sights set on the 2004 NASCAR Nextel Cup season championship.
Sam Sharpe

Wanted: Psychic. Must be able to predict the unpredictable. First assignment will be to determine the 2004 Nextel Cup champion and top 15 in points. Pay will depend on ability to accurately predict all 15 positions.

No, I didn't call in the ghost of Jeane Dixon or consult a Ouija board to make my predictions for the 2004 Nextel Cup points race, but I might wish I had done both when the end of the year rolls around.

There are simply more variables in NASCAR racing than in any major sport. That's the nature of the game. In what other sport do you have 43 men hurling themselves around in metal boxes at 150 to 200 miles per hour, just inches apart? Needless to say, there's a lot of room for unforeseen problems and scenarios. Merely a couple of bobbles at inopportune times last season and Matt Kenseth's run to the 2003 Winston Cup title could have been derailed.

With that in mind, I took a stab at predicting the finishing order of the top 15 in the chase for the inaugural Nextel Cup. At least a dozen teams are capable of claiming the title, but one stands out as a clear favorite.

In two seasons of competition in NASCAR's top division, Jimmie Johnson has demonstrated the mettle required to become a champion. His performance over the last half of the season was a model of consistency, as no driver on the circuit scored more points in the final six races. Glance over the final 10 races and Johnson and crew chief Chad Knaus showed why they are one of the top combinations in the sport. The No. 48 Lowe's Chevrolet recorded one win, three 2nds, three 3rds, a 7th, an 8th, and a 34th in the final 10 races. That performance allowed Johnson to move within 90 points of Kenseth at the end of the season.

Johnson waves to
the crowd during
driver introductions
at the Bud Shootout.
Sam Sharpe

Others who will factor heavily into the title chase are Kevin Harvick, Jeff Gordon, and Ryan Newman. No driver in the sport gained more in the points race last season than Harvick, who moved 16 spots, from 21st to 5th, between the 2002 and 2003 campaigns. Gordon, like Johnson, had a strong finish to last season, getting two wins in the final five races and finishing fourth in points. Plus, he's won four titles already and will be a fixture in the title hunt for years to come. Newman, of course, won more races (8) than any driver last season, but he also had six DNFs, too many to seriously contend for the championship.

There are, of course, other drivers who could slip into contention during 2004. About the only thing predictable in recent seasons is that we won't see a repeat champion. No driver has successfully defended his title since Gordon won back-to-back Cups in 1997 and 1998, and of the last five champions—Dale Jarrett, Bobby Labonte, Gordon, Tony Stewart, and Kenseth—only Gordon had previously won a title. That's four first-time winners in five years.

Add it all up and Jimmie Johnson has the look of a Nextel Cup champion, and 2004 will be his year. Just ask my crystal ball.

Under the lights during the Bud Shootout, Johnson battles with Jamie McMurray (42), Kevin Harvick (29), Jeff Gordon (24), Dale Earnhardt Jr. (8), and Dave Blaney (23).
Sam Sharpe

Here Johnson takes on Mike Skinner (10), Ryan Newman (12), Dave Blaney (23), and eventual winner Dale Jarrett (88) in the Bud Shootout.
Sam Sharpe

The first of the two Gatorade Twin 125s gets underway at Daytona to set the field for the Daytona 500. *Sam Sharpe*

1—Jimmie Johnson

Look for Johnson's 2003 momentum to carry over into this season, his third in NASCAR's top division. (Could that be possible?) All he's done in his first two seasons is finish fifth in points and grab three wins during his rookie season, then finish second in points and take three more victories last season [2003]. Johnson didn't win in 2003 until May when he won at Lowe's Motor Speedway, but expect the team to begin 2004 with a flourish, getting at least two wins by the time the 600 rolls around at Charlotte. Few teams in the sport have the talent behind the wheel, the crew chief, the chemistry, and the backing that the No. 48 Lowe's team possesses. Look for Hendrick Motorsports, an organization that's won five Cup titles over the past decade, to add a sixth in 2004 as Johnson and crew chief Chad Knaus win the inaugural Nextel Cup.

2003: 3 wins, 14 top 5s, 20 top 10s, 2nd in points

Key Stats: Johnson has spent 69 consecutive weeks in the top 10 in NASCAR Winston Cup points, the longest current streak in the series and ninth longest streak in the modern era.

Johnson and Knaus
do a little Daytona
day-dreaming in
the garage area.
Sam Sharpe

Here, Johnson chats
with teenage
teammate Brian
Vickers in the garage
area at Daytona.
Sam Sharpe

When practice is over or getting ready to start, drivers stick close to the garage where the car is kept. Jimmie Johnson is no different. *Nigel Kinrade*

2—Kevin Harvick

After hitting the circuit with a bang in 2001—he was ninth in points and won twice—Harvick nearly fell from sight in 2002, finishing 21st in points and getting just one victory. That changed in 2003, however, as Harvick bounced back into the upper echelon of the sport. Sure, he again won just one race, but he had 18 top 10s and 11 top 5s and finished only 252 points out of first. Team owner Richard Childress hasn't had a top 5 in points since Dale Earnhardt was second in 2000, but Harvick will restore some of the old glory to the organization with a strong run this season.

2003: 1 win, 11 top 5s, 18 top 10s, 5th in points

Key stats: Harvick has completed 39 races without a DNF, dating to Atlanta in the fall of 2002.

The Lowe's crew makes some adjustments to the No. 48 car prior to the season's first big race—the Daytona 500.
Sam Sharpe

Ready to rock and roll at Daytona.
Sam Sharpe

3—Jeff Gordon

No driver led more laps in 2003 than Gordon and no driver today knows more about winning or contending for a championship. Gordon's worst points finish since his rookie season of 1993 is ninth, and he'll be strong again this season. (No surprise there, huh?) Eventually Gordon will get that coveted fifth points title, but it won't come this season as teammate/employee Johnson will steal his thunder. There's consolation in that, however, as Gordon is co-owner of Johnson's team.

2003: 3 wins, 15 top 5s, 20 top 10s, 4th in points

Key stats: Gordon has finished in the top 10 in Cup points for 10 consecutive seasons, including 7 seasons in the top 5.

4—Ryan Newman

OK, we know he won more races (eight) than any driver on the circuit last season, but when did Penske Racing last win the Cup championship? Answer: It's never happened. Newman will be strong again in 2004 but not strong enough to garner a title. His 17 top 5s last season were the most in Winston Cup, but he also had six DNFs, dooming his chances for a better points finish. Don't be surprised to see Newman among the leaders in wins again. This kid will give Roger Penske his first Cup title someday. Just not this year.

2003: 8 wins, 17 top 5s, 22 top 10s, 6th in points

Key stats: 8 wins, 11 poles. Enough said.

5—Matt Kenseth

Kenseth was Mr. Consistency last season, collecting 25 top 10s and finishing 30th or worse only three times. Look for more wins from this team in 2004. Also expect more bad racing luck. He'll rebound nicely, though, for a strong points finish.

While most of the country is still buried under snow and ice, another season gets under way at Daytona. The Lowe's crew pushes its steed toward the grid on qualifying day. *Sam Sharpe*

2003: 1 win, 11 top 5s, 25 top 10s, 1st in points

Key stats: Kenseth's blown engine at Homestead-Miami relegated his No. 17 Dewalt team to a last-place finish in the season finale. Did someone say the party's over?

6—Dale Earnhardt Jr.

Junior became a bona fide championship contender last season and can be expected to remain among the top drivers in the sport. The points championship that will lift him to a whole new plateau in NASCAR will have to wait, though.

2003: 2 wins, 13 top 5s, 21 top 10s, 3rd in points

Key stats: Junior's points finishes in four Cup seasons are an up-and-down: 16th, 8th, 11th, and 3rd.

7—Tony Stewart

Is there a more talented driver in the sport than Stewart, who has won championships in everything he's driven? Probably not. Don't expect another championship for the No. 20 team this year, however, as Lowe's and Johnson pull even—at least on the track—with Stewart and Home Depot in the battle for hardware store supremacy.

2003: 2 wins, 12 top 5s, 18 top 10s, 7th in points

Key stats: Remarkably, last season's finish of 7th was Stewart's worst points finish in five seasons, and he'll match that in 2004.

Jimmie Johnson has the pedal to the floor during qualifying for the Daytona 500. *Sam Sharpe*

8—Bobby Labonte

Labonte regained a little of his old rhythm last season with new crew chief Michael "Fatback" McSwain calling the shots. After slipping to 16th in the 2002 points rundown, he more than doubled his number of top-5 and top-10 finishes from that season to 2003.

2003: 2 wins, 12 top 5s, 17 top 10s, 8th in points

Key stats: In his nine seasons with Joe Gibbs Racing, Labonte has finished in the top 10 in points seven times. Expect another in 2004.

9—Terry Labonte

Who is this guy, some interloper into the top 10 of the points standings? No, he's a two-time (1984, 1996) Winston Cup champion who has rediscovered his rhythm. Labonte won the final Labor Day race at Darlington last fall and recorded his first top-10 points finish since a ninth in 1998.

2003: 1 win, 4 top 5s, 9 top 10s, 10th in points

Key stats: Labonte's streak of 42 consecutive races without a DNF, dating from Talladega in October 2002, is the longest current streak in the series.

After qualifying, Johnson jumps out of the Lowe's Chevy in the impound area just before the car's technical inspection.
Sam Sharpe

On the way back to the transporter, Johnson is cornered by ever-present media members. Media attention is at its height during the two-week odyssey known as Speedweeks in Daytona. *Sam Sharpe*

This is what is called a debriefing. Chad Knaus (left) and Jimmie Johnson talk about what the car was doing and how to make it better. *Sam Sharpe*

Team discussions can take place anywhere. Brian Vickers (left) and Johnson chat while standing up against Matt Kenseth's car in the garage at Daytona. *Sam Sharpe*

10—Robby Gordon

Gordon has been around NASCAR since 1991 but last year marked just his second full season as a Cup driver. Think he's had time to figure it out yet? This pick is a testament to the strength of Richard Childress Racing—and to Gordon's driving ability, which will be evident this year like never before.

2003: 2 wins, 4 top 5s, 10 top 10s, 16th in points

Key stats: Gordon is 35 and entering his third full season with Childress—the same age and juncture with the Childress team that Dale Earnhardt began to put his stamp on the sport.

11—Brian Vickers

Think Tony Stewart. Think Jimmie Johnson. Think Ryan Newman. This kid—he's only 20—will be fast right off the truck at Daytona and will turn in a 2004 performance reminiscent of the rookie seasons of the aforementioned drivers.

2003: Won three times on the way to the Busch Series championship

Key stats: Vickers has demonstrated the ability to win at every level, becoming the youngest ever winner in the Hooters ProCup Series at age 16 and winning the Busch title less than a month after turning 20.

While involved in a discussion with his teammate, Johnson picks at a roof flap on top of his machine. *Sam Sharpe*

When two drivers get together, chances are a third will come walking by and join in. Here, Mark Martin adds to the discussion between Johnson and Vickers. *Sam Sharpe*

12—Kurt Busch

Don't be blinded by the obnoxious behavior of NASCAR's reigning bad boy. Busch, despite his off-track shenanigans, can flat drive a race car. The No. 97 team began to slip in the latter part of 2003, though, and don't expect a quick turnaround.

2003: 4 wins, 9 top 5s, 14 top 10s, 11th in points

Key stats: After winning at Bristol last August, Busch had only one top 5 and three top 10s in the final 12 races. The string included finishes of 38th, 40th, 41st, 39th, and 36th.

13—Jamie McMurray

McMurray didn't reach victory lane in 2003, but he turned in a solid Rookie of the Year performance. Although he won't burn up the track this season, expect more good things from this team, like the pole McMurray claimed in the season finale at Homestead.

2003: 0 wins, 5 top 5s, 13 top 10s, 13th in points

Key stats: McMurray finished third in the Brickyard 400 and had eight more top-10 finishes in the final 15 races, including a third at Bristol and a fourth at Darlington in consecutive races.

14—Jeremy Mayfield

Mayfield and team owner Ray Evernham stayed together despite persistent rumors of an impending split much of last season. Mayfield has yet to regain his magic from 1998, though, when he won his first race and finished seventh in points with Penske Racing. He made strides last season, nonetheless.

2003: 0 wins, 4 top 5s, 12 top 10s, 19th in points

Key stats: Mayfield has recorded only six top 5s and 16 top 10s in two seasons with Evernham. His numbers with Penske in 1998 were 12 top 5s and 16 top 10s. His points finishes since then have been 11th, 24th, 35th, 26th, and 19th.

Taking it easy in the old office chair, Jimmie grabs some contemplation time before going to work. *Nigel Kinrade*

Rusty Wallace holds off Jimmie Johnson and Matt Kenseth during 2004 Daytona Speedweeks action.
Sam Sharpe

15—Dale Jarrett

The woes that befell Robert Yates Racing last year didn't happen overnight and they won't go away overnight either. Jarrett's performance won't be quite as dismal this season, however, as he attempts to claw his way back up the ladder.

2003: 1 win, 1 top 5, 7 top 10s, 26th in points

Key stats: Last season's finish of 26th in points was Jarrett's worst in his nine seasons with Yates, and it broke a string of seven consecutive top 10s.

In a big pack of traffic during the Daytona 500, Johnson battles with Ken Schrader (49), Ryan Newman (12), Kasey Kahne (9), Kurt Busch (97), and teammate Brian Vickers (25).
Sam Sharpe

Here polesitter Greg Biffle (16) leads Johnson, Sterling Marlin (40), and Casey Mears (41) during the season-opening Daytona 500 in 2004.
Sam Sharpe

WHAT'S NEW

Nextel became the new title sponsor of NASCAR's top division at the end of 2003 when R. J. Reynolds and its Winston brand ended a 32-year association with the sanctioning body. The Winston Cup now becomes the Nextel Cup. Look for lots of yellow and black and very little red and white on the circuit this season.

Sunoco will replace Unocal and its Union 76 brand as the official fuel supplier of NASCAR, ending another long-term relationship. Is there a pattern here?

NASCAR has decreed that teams must run a smaller rear spoiler this season, taking downforce from the cars. Goodyear will respond with a softer compound for its tires, allowing more grip and offsetting the loss of downforce.

Ford gained approval last year for a new engine cylinder head to be used in 2004. The head has a larger intake port that will allow the blue oval engine builders to better compete with the General Motors SB2 head and the P7 of the Dodge. Ford's previous cylinder head design had been used in NASCAR since 1992.

Ford will debut a new Taurus this season as well, complete with a new nose and tail section. Wood Brothers Racing built the prototype and Dale Jarrett tested it at Atlanta in August, when the Woods' driver, Ricky Rudd, couldn't make the test date.

Sometimes, getting to the racetrack is more difficult than driving around it, as evidenced by the traffic pattern through the garage at Daytona. *Sam Sharpe*

Above and opposite: Getting ready to race is a pretty involved process. Getting in, strapping up, buckling this and fastening that, it all takes a while, but the result is a driver ready to race. *Sam Sharpe*

A multitude of emotions flicker over Jimmie Johnson's face during a brief time in the garage area at Daytona International Speedway. *Sam Sharpe*

One sentimental favorite to win the race battles one of the odds-on favorites for the season title in the early laps of the 2004 Daytona 500. Rusty Wallace (2) did not win the Daytona 500, but Johnson was a contender for the season title again. *Sam Sharpe*

Mark Martin (6), John Andretti, and Johnson battle through the tri-oval at Daytona in 2004. *Sam Sharpe*

Here, Michael Waltrip leads Sterling Marlin, Johnson, and Mark Martin during the race. *Sam Sharpe*

Happy times in the garage at Daytona, getting the season off to a good start. *Sam Sharpe*

Eventual third place finisher Scott Wimmer rides behind Johnson at Daytona. *Sam Sharpe*

CAREER STATISTICS

PERSONAL

Birthdate: Sept. 17, 1975 (El Cajon, Calif.)
Resides: Cornelius, North Carolina
Height: 5 feet 11 inches
Weight: 160 pounds
Marital status: Single

NASCAR CUP SERIES CAREER SUMMARY

Season	Races	Wins	Top 5	Top 10	Poles	Points	Rank
2001	3	0	0	0	0	210	52
2002	36	3	6	21	5	4600	5
2003	36	3	14	20	2	4932	2
Totals	75	6	20	41	7		

NASCAR BUSCH SERIES CAREER SUMMARY

Season	Races	Wins	Top 5	Top 10	Poles	Points	Rank
1999	5	0	0	1	0	521	63
2000	31	0	0	6	0	3264	10
2001	33	1	4	9	0	3871	8
Totals	69	1	4	16	0		

ASA CAREER SUMMARY

Season	Races	Wins	Top 5	Top 10	Poles	Rank
1997	3	0	0	1	0	46
1998	20	0	6	15	1	4
1999	20	2	9	14	3	3
Totals	43	2	15	30	4	

ASA CAREER WIN SUMMARY

Date	Race Name	Track
6/12/1999	Greased Lightning 200	Memphis Motorsports Park
10/2/1999	NC Sweet Potato 400	Orange County Speedway

OFF-ROAD CHAMPIONSHIPS

MTEG Stadium Series, Grand National Trucks (3) 1992–94
Short-Course Off-Road Enthusiasts (SCORE) (1) 1994
Short-Course Off-Road Drivers Association Winter Series (2) 1996-97

OFF-ROAD HIGHLIGHTS

More than 25 victories and 100 podium finishes in off-road career

INDEX

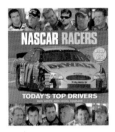
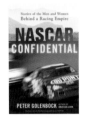
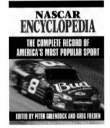
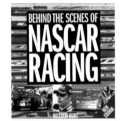

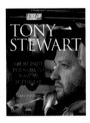